Bosque Bonito

Violent Times along the Borderland during the Mexican Revolution

Map of area drawn by W.D. Smithers.

Bosque Bonito

Violent Times along the Borderland during the Mexican Revolution

Robert Keil

edited by
Elizabeth McBride

Sul Ross State University
A Member of the Texas State University System

Center for Big Bend Studies
Occasional Papers No. 7
Alpine, Texas

ISBN 0-9707709-0-1

Center for Big Bend Studies
Occasional Papers No. 7

Kelly S. García, *Technical Editor*
Robert J. Mallouf, *Series Editor*

To Robana
In appreciation for forty good years
we spent together

Table of Contents

Editor's Introduction

Mexican History on the Border in the Early Twentieth Century

From the time the Spaniards arrived in Mexico to the present, the country has suffered a tumultuous history. But it wasn't until the nineteenth century that the Native Americans (the indigenous peoples), the Creoles (those of Spanish blood born in Mexico), and the *mestizos* (those of mixed Spanish and Native-American blood), began to rebel against the Spanish authorities.

The Mexican War of Independence was launched in 1810 by a priest named Miguel Hidalgo y Costillo. Hidalgo captured Acapulco and declared Mexico independent of Spanish rule. The revolution spread through Guanajuato and Guadalajara before it ended with the execution of Hidalgo by the Spanish in 1811. But by then, Mexico was bent on revolution, and Hidalgo was succeeded by another priest, José Mariá Morelos y Pavón.

Morelos' program of reform contained three primary goals: equal rights for ethnic groups, the end of special rights for the army and the Roman Catholic Church, and the end to the large estates, which he wanted broken up and awarded as small land grants to the Mexican people for farming.

A series of conflicts ensued between the liberals, those in favor of returning the land to the people, and the conservatives, those who opposed this process, which lasted until 1822, when two opposing leaders, Augustín de Iturbide and Vincente Guererro, came to an agreement and called jointly for independence.

In 1823, after a revolt led by General Antonio López de Santa Anna, one of Iturbide's former officers, Mexico became a republic and embraced freedom. The people wrote a constitution that established a Congress consisting of two houses and elected Guadalupe Victoria as Mexico's first president.

Still, throughout the century, conflicts and struggles rocked the country, with Santa Anna switching loyalties back and forth from one political leader to another. Then, in 1835, Texans rebelled against Santa Anna. Although Santa Anna prevailed at the Battle of the Alamo, the conflict was settled in Texas' favor at the Battle of San Jacinto, where Santa Anna's troops were defeated.

To save himself, Santa Anna signed a treaty granting independence to a large area of Mexico's territory. Nevertheless, the hostilities along the border continued, leading to an attack in April 1846 by American forces and a declaration of war against Mexico.

The treaty of Guadalupe Hidalgo, signed in 1848, ended the war, ceding to the United States all of California, Nevada and Utah, most of Arizona, and parts of Colorado, New Mexico, and Wyoming. Texas was recognized as part of the United States all the way to the Rio Grande. In 1853, the United States acquired even more land from Mexico through the Gadsden Purchase, paying $10 million for southern Arizona and New Mexico.

After the war with the United States, politics in Mexico remained chaotic. The patterns of conflict continued throughout the nineteenth century until Benito Juárez, a Zapotec Indian who promoted the return of land to the people, offered leadership. But after the invasion by France, Great Britain, and Spain, Napoleon declared Maximilian of Hapsburg, brother of the Austrian emperor, emperor of Mexico.

In 1867, after Juárez' forces captured and executed Maximilian, the republic was restored. Then, in still a later revolution, Porfirio Díaz, a *mestizo* general, took power as a conservative, controlled Mexico with his troops, and ruled until 1911, allowing no effective opposition.

Thus it was that Mexico entered the twentieth century with a stable but repressive government. Díaz remained president for more than thirty years, until he was overthrown by Francisco Madero in 1911, after a year of violent revolution. Power then passed to Venustiano Carranza, but his position was constantly challenged in the second decade of the twentieth century by the revolutionary activities of Francisco "Pancho" Villa and Emiliano Zapata. It is at this dangerous and chaotic point in the history of relations between the United States and Mexico that Robert Keil's story begins.

American History on the Border in the Early Twentieth Century

By 1913, the violence originating in Mexico as a result of the revolution was affecting Americans who lived along the border in Texas, New Mexico, and Arizona. The first of many violent episodes occurred on January 23, 1913, when Customs Inspector Joe Sitters interrupted a wake on the Texas side of the Rio Grande in search of a notorious bandit named Chico Cano. Cano was a colorful and complicated figure who, in spite of his bloody career as a cattle and horse thief, was also well liked by many Texans and was, for a time, friendly with Captain Leonard

Matlack of the U.S. Cavalry. Like all the incidents in the Big Bend during the early part of the century, the facts surrounding Cano's activities remain murky.[1]

In the gunfight between Sitters' group and Chico Cano's gang, Cano escaped, but John Simpson Howard, a customs inspector, was killed, and Joe Sitters and other companions were wounded. From this time until the 1920s, when the violence subsided, the people of the Big Bend were victims of numerous violent incidents perpetrated by both Mexicans and Texans.

During that time, the violence in the state of Chihuahua, Mexico, drove refugees to cross the river at Ojinaga. On December 5, Troop E of the Fifteenth Cavalry arrived in Presidio to assist in processing the refugees, who were walked from Presidio to Marfa in a journey that began on January 14, 1914, and took three days for the twelve-mile-long column of refugees to complete.[2] Concurrently, wealthy Mexicans were fleeing with cash, among them the owner of the Terrazas ranch, General Luis Terrazas.[3]

It became a scene of tragic chaos. While the Red Cross was in Ojinaga to assist the refugees, Mexican Federalists were battling rebels in the very same city. Francisco "Pancho" Villa took the garrison in Ojinaga on January 10, and the Federalists surrendered to the U.S. forces for protection.[4] With Texas and the U.S. government in disagreement about who was responsible for maintaining peace on the border, incidents of dramatic violence led to a bill introduced by Senator Claude Hudspeth of El Paso on February 2, 1915, appropriating $10,000 to expand the Texas Rangers, the official law enforcement body of the state.

On May 23, 1915, another border tragedy occurred when Joe Sitters and Texas Ranger Gene Hulen were murdered in Mexico by Mexican bandits. When the two posses that had been formed reached the victims, they found the bodies shattered and mutilated. It was believed that Chico Cano was responsible for the massacre.[5]

During this time, in spite of the increased numbers of Rangers and the presence of Troops G and F of the U.S. Cavalry at Camp Marfa,[6] the violence continued.

Rangers were being killed, and the Mexicans who were captured by the Rangers were either being killed (the Rangers claimed) while trying to escape, or simply disappearing.[7] "Ranger Captain Monroe Fox stated that the situation along the Texas-Mexican border in the Big Bend country was out of hand; that thieves and bandits were operating in large numbers."[8] The argument over the responsibility for maintaining peace on the border continued, but by February 1, 1916, an estimated eight thousand U.S. troops were on duty along the Mexican border.[9]

The attitude of the United States changed when, on the night of March 9, 1916, a large Mexican force crossed the Rio Grande and attacked the small town of Columbus, New Mexico, killing sixteen Americans and burning the town. It was believed the raid was led by Francisco "Pancho" Villa, the leader of the revolution in Mexico. After the Columbus raid, the United States sent troops of the Sixth Cavalry on what was called the First Punitive Expedition, commanded by General John J. Pershing, into Mexico on March 16, 1916. They pursued Villa in Mexico for two years without success.

This military maneuver emptied the border area of troops and increased tension between the U.S. and Mexico.[10] As American and Mexican officials worked to find a solution,[11] another attack occurred on May 5, 1916, this time at the candelilla wax plant at Glenn Springs, Texas. Mexican bandits killed four Americans, raided the store, and razed many of the buildings. While Glenn Springs was being attacked, a second group of bandits struck the little mining camp of Boquillas, about twenty miles southeast of the wax plant.[12]

In response to the Glenn Springs and Boquillas raids, the War Department ordered a full-scale military retaliation with the army supplying both men and machinery to the Big Bend area. Commanded by Major George T. Langhorne, Troops A and B of the Eighth Cavalry, sent from Fort Bliss, reached Marathon on May 8, and started for Glenn Springs.[13] At this time, Governor James E. Ferguson also increased the state's Ranger force by fifty men and ordered Ranger Captain Monroe Fox to investigate the Glenn Springs and Boquillas raids.[14]

The Second Punitive Expedition, which crossed the border at Boquillas on May 9, 1916,[15] placed Major Langhorne in Mexico concurrently with General Pershing, who was pursuing Villa. Langhorne crossed the border followed by Colonel Frederick W. Sibley from Fort Clark, and within a week, the forces had penetrated nearly two hundred miles south of the Rio Grande.[16] But this campaign, like the First Punitive Expedition, failed to achieve its goal, capturing only a few bandits before giving up after the other culprits had scattered.

By July of 1916, more than 150,000 troops were assembled along the Mexican border[17] and on July 13, in answer to an appeal by the government of Texas, the National Guard of New Mexico, Arizona, and Texas was sent to the Big Bend. It was estimated that fifty thousand regulars and 160,000 National Guard troops were actively patrolling the border at that time.[18] Camp Marfa, the central headquarters, became responsible for supplying twelve border outposts, many of which could be reached only by pack train. The nearest outpost was fifty-four miles away, but there were others as many as one hundred miles from Marfa.

In his book *Chronicles of the Big Bend,* photographer and cavalryman W. D. Smithers explains that it took a pack train three days to travel from Marfa to Lajitas. "Besides being the most difficult outpost to supply, Lajitas was one of the most strategic, for it guarded the western approach from Mexico to the quicksilver mines at Terlingua."[19]

American intervention had become a serious issue to Mexico. James L. Rogers, the United States Consul in Mexico City, planned a conference in El Paso between General Alvaro Obregón and General Hugh Scott on May 2, 1916, to negotiate a solution. In return for an assurance that Mexican forces would not engage the punitive forces, and that the government would begin a vigorous campaign against the bandits, the Americans promised "gradual withdrawal of all expeditionary forces."[20]

The conference attempted to resolve the hostility created when the sovereignty of both nations had been violated. The Mexican Revolution had caused constant strain on the border, and the Punitive Expedition of May 1916 violated the agreement reached by Scott and Obregón, leaving President Carranza in a difficult position, as his people were calling for him to "maintain the dignity of the nation and defend the autonomy of her soil."[21]

When President Wilson committed American troops to France in 1917, the number of cavalrymen on the border was reduced, and Langhorne's forces were unable to stop the banditry. In 1919, however, after the end of World War I, Maj. Gen. Charles T. Menhor, Chief of the Army Air Service, established an air patrol along the border. For approximately two years, this patrol aided the U.S. Cavalry. Although the air patrol increased hostility, relations between the United States and Mexico were eased in 1920 when the War Department reduced the cavalry on the border. At the same time, the Mexican Revolution reached its end, and President Obregón met his obligation to police the bandits on the Rio Grande.[22]

It was in those violent and confusing years between 1913 and 1920 that the incidents occurred which Robert Keil wrote of in *Bosque Bonito*.

Robert Keil and the *Bosque Bonito* Manuscript

Born in Dubois, Pennsylvania, in 1898, Robert Keil dreamed of joining the United States Cavalry, a goal which was realized when he ran away at the age of 15 and enlisted, changing his name from Kiel to Keil, lying about his age, and informing military officials he had no living relatives.

Keil had a deep affection for animals, particularly horses and mules, and loved working on the pack trains. After serving in the Eighth U.S. Cavalry on the border from 1913 to 1918, Keil remained in the Big Bend to work as a Civil Service packer for two additional years under Charley Coward, U.S. Army pack master.

For over six years, Robert Keil lived in the borderlands along the Rio Grande in the wild and primitive Big Bend country of West Texas. He was living the life he had longed for, and he himself said later that his years in the Big Bend were the happiest and wildest years of his life. Yet they were also years of violence, and he would remain haunted throughout his life by the tragedies he had witnessed. The beauty and tragedy of Keil's river experience were powerfully impressed upon him, and they continued to hold him captive as time and again he wrote the story and sought to have it published, and time and again, he was disappointed.

In Keil's later life, his one goal was to return to the area, and in 1963, forty years after his life in the Big Bend, he finally revisited the sites of events he had lived and witnessed when only a young boy. During his return, Keil moved step by step through the past, deeper and deeper into the wild beautiful bosque of the river he loved, reliving every event so powerfully imprinted in his memory. It was after that trip that Robert Keil revised the manuscript which eventually ended up at the Center for Big Bend Studies (CBBS).

The CBBS first acquired Robert Keil's 1963 manuscript from his daughter, Linda Davis, who recognized its historical importance and had made many attempts to see this document through to publication. Davis eventually submitted the manuscript to Melleta Bell, archivist of the Archives of the Big Bend, who in turn forwarded it to Robert Mallouf, director of the Center for Big Bend Studies at Sul Ross State University.

In the spring of 2001, I was hired by the CBBS to edit the manuscript. Robert Mallouf, Kelly García, CBBS editor, and I were in agreement that *Bosque Bonito* was a moving and valuable historical document, written with a sharp intelligence which combined emotion with power and insight. The manuscript was already familiar to Glenn Justice and Enrique Madrid, two historians of West Texas, and its authenticity was attested to by the accompanying photographs, notes, and letters his daughter provided.

It was thrilling to be entrusted with the Keil manuscript, an intelligently written document which offered not only the flavor of the early days of the twentieth century in Far West Texas, but also significant sociological information about the lives of both Mexicans and Americans during that time, as well as their interactions. More importantly, the manuscript provided first-hand accounts of the border violence in Pancho Villa's time through a powerful narrative having a specificity that was captivating.

Keil's testament offered new interpretations of the troubles along the border, interpretations that, although familiar in Big Bend oral history, had not been represented formally in written history. In Keil's narrative, the border violence took on a complexity that had never before been fully explored in a reliable historical document.

My first task as manuscript editor was to get in touch with Linda Davis, Robert Keil's daughter. Davis and I joined a tour of sites along the border led by Joyce Means, who grew up on the border and is herself a chronicler of the Big Bend.[23] Seeing for ourselves the hushed beauty of the country that Keil had written of with such eloquence, and the mass grave at Porvenir, where the Mexicans had buried the victims of the massacre which so affected him, we began to journey with him, asking ourselves: What was it like, what *could* it have been like, for such a young boy to be first transported from the eastern U.S. and exposed to the almost surreal, wild beauty of Far West Texas, and then deeply traumatized by the violence he witnessed in this untamed land? It was on that trip that the manuscript came fully to life for Davis, and through her reactions and her stories about her father, for me also.

I would like to thank Robert Mallouf and Kelly García for their help and support with this text, as well as for their advice in making editorial decisions, and Elizabeth Will of the Center's staff for her gracious willingness to perform time-consuming tasks of typing and scanning. I am grateful to all those who read the text before publication and offered suggestions, especially Enrique Madrid, Glenn Justice, Glenn Willeford, and Gerald Raun for the generous gift of their time.

The Big Bend is wild and sparsely populated, but rich in history. It is sometimes difficult for those who live in other parts of the country to grasp the interactions between Texans and Mexicans or to imagine a culture in which Mexican Americans wade through the shoals, drive a vehicle through the shallow water, or even walk across a dry riverbed from Texas to Chihuahua, Mexico, to have Sunday dinner with their Mexican grandparents.

As a friend once told me about the Big Bend, "This ain't Texas and this ain't Mexico. This is somethin' else."

Elizabeth McBride
Marfa, Texas
September 2001

Chapter 1—Memory

Memory is a strange thing. Sometimes it hits me like a winter storm, while at other times it feels soothing and pleasant, like the sweet smell of springtime on gentle breezes. Every living man who experienced the thrill and excitement of the Mexican border during the revolution has only to close his eyes to smell the pungent odor of mesquite and cornhusk fires, or the overpowering fragrance of roasting chiles. He can also hear through the long nights the wild lonely yells emitting from throats seared with fiery tequila. It was a time I would gladly return to, when modern conveniences were unknown, the time of huge cattle ranches, fine saddle horses, and mule pack trains—now forever gone.

Nothing stirs my memory more than the call of a mourning dove and I cannot recall one tragic incident that was not preceded by that mournful cry. It is eerie and weird, and when danger lurks in the night, it can cause brave men to step softly. Next only to the dove call in its power to take me back are the smells. Perhaps the mental faculty of memory and the sense of smell are strong in all men and certainly, as I become older, I am more conscious of them.

I believe that every happy event of my lifetime was accompanied by sweet and pleasant smells. The smell of bread baking reminds me of my mother and brings me a feeling of security. Sometimes a smell arouses a long-forgotten pleasure. The smell of a river with the sound of gentle splashing pulls my memory like a magnet to the Rio Grande and the Big Bend country of West Texas.

But smells can also signal danger, and those smells have saved many lives. On two occasions, the acrid smell of powder-smoke has hung over me, clearing only to reveal the deathly features of a human being lying sprawled before me on the ground. In both instances, I was but a witness—however, since then, the smell of gun-smoke has been a warning to me. It has been synonymous with death, blood, and suffering.

A great deal of the history of the Big Bend, and especially of the bosque country, has never been truthfully told, possibly because the true story, although familiar to many people who have lived along the river, violently contradicts the explanations that have been accepted into written history. I have never read of the border incidents in their true perspective. Yet it would be hard to dream up fictional events more sensational than the true ones that took place in 1917, 1918, and

1919. I have waited all these years for the story to be told, and now I will tell it myself. I am going to do my damnedest.

Chapter 2—Mexican Uprisings and the Bosque

In 1911, Porfirio Díaz, president of Mexico, was overthrown by Francisco Madero after a year of violent revolution. Díaz had been a president for the rich, always managing to take special care of the wealthy in every conceivable manner, but principally by special concessions and land grants. During the long years of Díaz' rule, the wealthy piled up riches while the peons were pushed further and further into the depths of poverty.

Understanding the threat offered by the desperation of the poor, President Díaz had created the Frontier Police or Rurales, an army made up of mercenaries from around the world. In the Mexican state of Chihuahua, they served under Chief Kosterlitzsky who had been a colonel in the army of Poland. Each man in the force was personally picked by Mr. Díaz, and although each had a great many special qualifications, principally they had to be tough, and if contemporary accounts can be believed, they were tough indeed.

Nevertheless, opposition to Díaz began to grow. Francisco I. Madero, a liberal landowner, became popular, but lost the election to Díaz in 1910. In November of that year, Madero called for rebellion as the only way to overthrow the oppression of the Díaz regime. By defeating federal troops, destroying railroads, and attacking towns and estates, Madero took power, forcing Díaz to flee Mexico.

It might have seemed that the troubles were over, for Mexico rejoiced when Díaz was ousted. For a short time the people seemed happy under Madero's leadership, but his weakness as a politician aroused, on the one side, the desire for another dictatorship and, on the other, a cry for greater reform. By then, the country was politicized, and would continue to turn to revolutionists for relief from their struggles.

In 1913, General Victoriano Huerta of the Mexican Army took power. But after Huerta executed Madero, Madero's followers organized behind Venustiano Carranza, a landowner with whom President Woodrow Wilson of the United States also sided. Carranza occupied Mexico City and Huerta fled. By then, revolutions were erupting all over Mexico, and Emiliano Zapata and Francisco "Pancho" Villa continued to challenge Carranza. Violence reached an all-time high, and relationships with the United States became hostile.

During this time the revolutionists, Zapata and Villa, kept Carranza engaged in fighting. Their tumultuous uprisings lead to tension on the border, and alienated the Texans, whose resentment intensified with the Carranza regime's illegal seizure of every American enterprise in Mexico.

Because Texans felt endangered, the state requested a cavalry regiment to protect its people along the Texas-Mexico border. This request was granted, and for many years, American troops patrolled all of the vast border area from Bosque Bonito to Brownsville, Texas. This was how I came to be assigned to the Eighth U.S. Cavalry along the Rio Grande.

The bosque, the country that I am most familiar with, lies south of Van Horn and extends fifty miles east of Presidio, Texas. The distance of roughly 125 miles averages twenty-five miles in width, taking in the Rim Rock, and runs down to the river. Just north of the bosque, going west on US 90 from Sanderson, lie the towns of Marathon, Alpine, Marfa, Valentine, and then Van Horn, all about thirty minutes apart, the distance the train could travel at that time before it required additional water. Of course, every native from Van Horn to Del Rio will tell you they live in the Big Bend. But my story does not touch the locale of what is now Big Bend National Park, below Marathon, which lies far to the east and downriver from the country I know.

With the exception of the area near the trails, you could say that all of this vast wilderness is unexplored, and I believe that my outfit might have explored more of it than anyone else before or since. It is a wild, strange country, uninhabited and lonely, principally because there are few roads.

Try to picture an area of more than fifteen thousand square miles with hundreds of canyons, almost two hundred mountain peaks of four thousand feet in elevation, sixty peaks of five thousand feet, fifteen peaks of seventy-five hundred feet, and at least three of eight thousand feet. More than half of the Big Bend's area is rough mountains, deep treacherous canyons, and inaccessible sheer walls of rock. The land is dry and barren, wild and spooky, but in almost every canyon and on many of the high ridges there are sweet springs of water. In a few places near the Rio Grande there are some of the largest hot springs in America.

Five miles east of Van Horn, which sits at the intersection of US 90 and IH 10, a high mountain range appears to the south, running eastward for almost a hundred miles, having the appearance of a monstrous rock wall built by human hands. This is the famous Rim Rock of the Upper Big Bend, a range of rock that is awe-inspiring.

In all of this vast area, only two roads cross the Rim Rock from towns inland to the river, one from Marfa via Brite's Ranch to Candelaria, and the other from Marfa to Presidio through Pinto Canyon. And in 120 miles, only two passable trails cross the Rim Rock toward the river.

To me, the hundreds of trails in the Upper Big Bend were always intriguing, especially those that led all the way into Chihuahua, Mexico. A trail is more than a path upon which one travels. It is a connection, a trade route, as well as an assistance to communication. Northern Mexico and the Big Bend have been traveled by mounted men continuously for the last four hundred years, and it is staggering to try to visualize the thousands of hooves responsible for some of the old deep trails.

On both sides of the thick bosque[24] there is a well-beaten trail that follows the river. The one on the Mexico side, called the "San Antone" Trail, runs from Pilares through San Antonio del Bravo and down to Ojinaga. During the revolution, as many as thirty-six thousand animals may have passed a given point between Juárez and Ojinaga in Chihuahua, and El Paso and Presidio in Texas. During the course of a year, that would add up to a 144,000 hooves chopping away at what was nothing but solid rock. At one place east of the small village of Bosque Bonito, the trail is cut to a depth of two feet into the rock, yet those revolutionary days added only about two inches to its depth.

As late as 1880, the fierce Apaches still dominated the Rim Rock country. It is surely a big, silent country, lonely and desolate, with mourning doves and hoot owls lending to its spookiness. In my time there, large bands of horses, mules, and burros ran everywhere. The country contained droves of domesticated hogs gone wild that lived in the bosque and stuck close to it. The old boars were something to stay away from. From experience, I learned that these hogs are more dangerous than javelinas.[25]

From the Rim Rock, all of the country drains toward the Rio Grande, a constant succession of canyons, cliffs, and ridges terminating at the river. Between the ridges there is rich soil on both sides. All the villages had garden plots that would grow almost anything, but the principal crops were beans, corn, chiles, and watermelons. Every village and town had a compound where meetings and dances were held. The houses, or jacales, were built by erecting ocotillo poles and plastering them with mud, and often included a *ramada,* or supported covering, that extended out from the building to provide shade.

Bosque Bonito is only a spot on the Rio Grande thirty-five miles south of Van Horn, Texas. When I first saw it, there were two small adobes on the Texas side, and a couple of similar buildings across the river in the state of Chihuahua. Nowhere else in Texas that I know of does the jojoba tree grow, bearing an edible, life-saving nut called a goat nut, or the pitaya, a cactus that bears a thorny fruit which, when red-ripe, falls off at a touch, looking and tasting exactly like a strawberry.

Almost all my time in that country was spent on the Rio Grande between Bosque Bonito and Candelaria. Big Bend National Park is 150 miles east of Candelaria, near Lajitas and Terlingua. In between were the towns of Ruidosa, Indio, Polvo, and Presidio, and the small settlements of Porvenir and Pilares. Today, there are a few new settlements, but all of the old river towns except Presidio are now ghost towns.[26]

The name Bosque Bonito, meaning pretty grove or forest, meant also the entire area along the Rio Grande. It may seem like a false description of the land when we consider the events of the story, most of which are ugly. Yet the bosque is closely connected to almost every part of the events, and so, because the river is always in my thoughts, I have called my story by its name.[27]

Chapter 3—Banditry along the Border

In addition to numerous mining companies, there were several huge ranches in the northern state of Chihuahua across the river from Texas, the primary two being the Terrazas Land and Cattle Company, and the T.O. Ranch. The T.O. Ranch was owned by a packing company from Chicago that controlled thirty thousand square miles and many thousands of cattle, sheep, and horses. It employed four hundred cowboys, over half of whom were Texans. The five towns, or camps, on the ranch were occupied by cowboys and their families, who did most of their purchasing of essentials on the ranch itself. The Terrazas outfit was owned by Luis Terrazas, a Mexican citizen who employed many Americans. Both of these ranches were a great deal larger than the great King Ranch of Texas fame.

The seizure of American property in Chihuahua turned hundreds of Americans against Mexico, and their resentment expanded to include the United States government, which refused to intervene with force to restore their property and their jobs. It was my privilege to know a few of the men who worked on the T.O. Ranch while it operated, and to have seen quite a lot of it myself. Although what I saw were only remnants of the old land holdings, it wasn't hard to visualize the vast amount of space the ranch occupied prior to 1911, with thousands of cattle everywhere.

When Mexico nationalized American properties, some of those who were notified to get out of Mexico or be shot, left. But others armed themselves, found hiding places, and waited, swearing that no "damned Mexican" would ever run them anywhere. A great many of these Texans actually became outlaws. From the beginning some were smart enough to band together for protection, and eventually all were working together in bands, raiding both in Texas and Mexico.

In the Mexican state of Chihuahua, the outlaws established their hideouts in mountains as rough and treacherous as any in North America. In Texas, they hid in the bosque because it was so sparsely populated, it had abundant water, and it could not be patrolled except on horseback. All of the men had to live, and although game was plentiful, those who didn't relish the life of Indians needed a great many things besides food. In a short time, most of the bolder ones became bandits and started stealing the things they needed. Then the people who lived on the border suffered a new kind of terror. Innocent citizens now feared not only the Mexican army, the revolutionaries, and the Rurales, but also the newly created communities of bandits.

The one constant fear that was shared, even by the Texas cowboys turned bandits, was of the Rurales, for everyone knew from experience of their superior marksmanship and their relentless determination to kill every bandit in Mexico. They were not scalp hunters, and not exactly bounty hunters, but each time a known bandit was killed, the Rural soldier responsible received ten extra pesos. It was thus that Carranza created their motivation.

The organized bandit gangs, it is true, were mostly Mexican, and even the Rurales had not been able to estimate their numbers. It has been suggested that in the state of Chihuahua alone there were six thousand active bandits.[28] Their numbers were made up of two-thirds army deserters from Villa and Carranza's forces, and one-third ex-cowboys and peons who had rebelled over one thing or another. The Texans, mostly cowboys, were believed to number over five hundred. A few of the bandits were mining men and soldiers of fortune. The latter came from every army of the world. When they left the armies of Mexico, in which they were barely subsisting, and took to the mountains as rogue bandits, a few became wealthy.

The outlaws were sometimes referred to as Villistas, but while their objectives were connected to those of the revolutionaries, they worked separately from both Carranza and Villa. They became armies within themselves. Every outlaw had to have a good fast horse, and except within towns or villages, they had only contempt for either Carranza or Villa foot soldiers.

It was known that three gangs were made up primarily of Texans, and a few others that were mixed—that is, Mexicans and Americans—operated around Corralitos and Casas Grandes in Central Chihuahua. In the mixed bands, the Texans were determined to boss. As long as there was a Mexican, camp work was not for Texans. The Texans hunted, but left the cooking, wood chopping, and dishwashing to the Mexicans. The Texans thought also that an American should be the gang leader. Many Mexican bandits were damn tough hombres, just as deadly as their Texas buddies, and disputes over these matters could lead to killings. By no means was it always the Mexican who died in his boots.

In many of the mixed gangs, Mexicans and Americans became friends, sharing everything except women, who were treated with less compassion than the horses. It was a good deal for the Mexicans because their American buddies almost always had a good horse and a fine, American-made saddle. At that time almost every Mexican rode a big-horned Chihuahua saddle with a flimsy maguey cinch and a grass rope for a bridle. With such an outfit, he could hardly rope a small calf without getting busted. The Americans also had good weapons, and if there was money in anybody's pocket, it was usually in the American's. Even his boots, hat, and clothing were the best, and if he was killed, his Mexican buddy naturally got the whole outfit.

An American outlaw was given a wide berth by Mexicans living in the villages and towns in Chihuahua, and Mexican outlaws meeting American outlaws in the bosque of Chihuahua didn't need the wave of a rifle barrel to inspire them to make a wide circle. Most outlaws during the revolution used both sides of the river, while a few never did leave Texas. It was impossible to tell who were outlaws and distinguish them positively from honest cowboys.

Gang leaders maintained their power by planning successive raids, but they also had to be good marksmen. Their code of ethics demanded that every man obey the leader, especially while raiding. When a man refused to obey, he was shot. That was the rule of the outlaw.

For a time, when the bandits were first active, hiding, fighting, and stealing were exciting to them, but they were soon bored. They loved to gamble, but few of them had money to lose. They loved women, but it wasn't easy to get them. Soon enough, women became a burning problem, and the combination of boredom, greed, and lust led to more terror.

In late 1916, in the towns of Corralitos, Casas Grandes, Colonia Juárez, Colonia Dublán, and San Domingo, it became a common and dreaded spectacle to see fifteen or twenty armed men racing toward the unresisting and terrified citizens, who at that time were the only honest working people in Chihuahua.

As the bandits approached from more than a mile away, they would start yelling and shooting, believing that terrorization was the first step in taking a village. By the time the bandits reached the town, all their guns would be empty and their horses winded. For a time, these attacks succeeded in keeping the villagers under control, but early in 1917, the town of Corralitos resisted, killing or wounding every single bandit in the raid, and the news of the slaughter gave all the other villages new courage and the gangs a new problem to worry over.

Until the defeat at Corralitos, the bandits had operated individually once they entered the villages. They would split up and steal anything they could find, even a likely girl, and whatever they carried off was theirs. After the Corralitos raid, the bandits were forced to change their procedure. They made quick raids and stayed united, allowing no man to yell or shoot before they reached the town. At a mile out, they stopped running their horses down. When they reached their hideout, everything taken except the girls would be equally divided. Then those who had no women would draw for the new ones.

Almost every girl stolen was young, and a great many had never been away from their homes before. A few didn't mind life in a bandit camp, but most of the victims had never before been molested in any way, and sooner or later they tried either to escape or kill themselves.

No ranch or village in the border area was safe, and soon every man began distrusting his neighbor. For those who lived on the assumption that the only good men in Mexico were dead ones, it became common practice to shoot them from ambush.

★ ★ ★

I lived in the area of the raids during the revolution and again in 1922 and 1923, having returned with a New Mexico cattle outfit that had secured pastures during the New Mexico drought. The cattle carried a war finance loan, and my father-in-law's two thousand cattle were part of the outfit. Every old-timer vividly remembered the bandit raids as well as the American bandits who were part of them. Many of the villages were raided as many as fifty times in two years. Both armies, federal and revolutionary, did a little raiding too, regardless of what they called it.

When Villa personally conducted a raid, he followed it up with a sort of street carnival and recruiting drive. After ransacking a town, Villa's officers would round the people up, and one of his men would speak in his behalf. Then his followers would cheer wildly, and if Villa was not busy at the time, the cheering would be his cue to gallop down the street, sweep off his hat, and smile broadly. He would then thank everyone for the loot that had been taken without permission.

Although he was not educated, Villa was no fool, and he possessed one thing that Carranza did not, which was an honest face. He always asked for recruits, and on each occasion a large number answered his plea, being promised arms and ammunition, food, clothing, and shoes, a payday, and above all else, a chance to be on the side that liberated the poor.

Those who had been living well before he came, but were carried away by his persuasiveness, soon found it would be a while before Villa would make good his promises, and they were faced with the certainty of being worse off than ever before. Recruits without guns (and few had one) would be asked if they didn't know a friend, some old man maybe, who owned a gun, but was too old to join the liberators. Those who knew of a gun would be sent to borrow it with a few of Villa's soldiers accompanying him. If the owner protested, his new comrades would give him a few seconds to think it over, but then, if he was stubborn, he would be shot. Then, since a dead man doesn't need much, the raiders would split his belongings.

Many recruits from the various armies, after starving for a few weeks and getting farther and farther away from home each day, would pick a dark night, steal everything they possibly could, including a horse, and make tracks toward the mountains. There they could fill their bellies with venison, make a pair of *huaraches* (sandals) out of the hide, and become bandits, which was a better life than that of a soldier. But those who turned to banditry soon found that they faced five terrible obstacles: the Rurales, the Federal troops, Villa's men, other bandits, and the certainty of being shot at when they raided a village.

There was a time in 1917 when no bandit raids were reported for three months. Each gang had at some time in the past been ambushed by other bandits. Coming home to their hideouts after a raid, they had been fired on. Sometimes a few were killed, and always, the sneaky thieves took all of the loot. Everyone who lived through one of those ambushes felt it wasn't fair—they had ridden a hundred miles and taken all of the risks, only to have a thief who had risked nothing steal their property.

This period without raids was a real break for the honest people of Chihuahua. Carranza's troops did little raiding, but when they did, the purpose was to punish the villages that had been friendly to Villa. They would execute a few men and then take everything to keep it from falling into Villa's hands.

On some occasions, horses were stolen. If an officer saw a likely horse and took it from a thief for his own use, he would search the man, and if money or valuables were found on his person, the officer would take that too, supposedly for safekeeping. Then the soldier would be severely reprimanded and demoted to a corporal.[29]

Terror was real in Chihuahua during the revolution, but during all of the six years that wrecked Chihuahua, only five raids were made on the Texas border. Four of these were right on the river, and the raid on Brite's Ranch was less than twenty miles inland. Perhaps you have read that hundreds of wild, yelling bandits pulled these raids, but the truth is, none of them involved over thirty men, and the average number was about twenty. Even more important, though, was that many believed the raids were planned and made after unbearable provocation by Texans.

During all of the border terror, I can think of only four Americans killed under mysterious circumstances in the vicinity of Presidio, and only one in Jeff Davis County, which makes a total of five. Three of the Americans killed were immigration officers and the other two were cowboys. Every one of the men were shot up and mutilated. It is my opinion that these men were killed from ambush, and that the ambushers were Mexicans, but there was never any physical evidence produced to prove it.

My fellow soldiers and I knew three of the victims well. One of the men had a sister who was close to a family in Valentine, a special friend of my girl there. He was one of the immigration officers. The cowboys, who were considered friends, had stayed at our camp many nights, where they were both popular and welcome. Even the officers seemed happy to have them there.

As I look back now, I see things more clearly than I did when I was twenty. I don't mean to make light of such awful crimes, but mutilation did not originate during this period. It was a custom that had been practiced by Americans in Texas and all over the Southwest for more than a hundred years. One of my relatives, a Ranger in Kerr County following the Civil War, had owned a quirt made from skinning a Comanche's back while he was still alive.

My opinion was that anyone could have murdered the five Americans, all of whom were killed in a short span of time. Two of the immigration officers had been killed together, while the other murders were single action jobs. The very loneliness of the country always seemed to add mystery and horror to the killings on the border. In spite of the many atrocities that followed the murders of the five men, every officer in Presidio and Jeff Davis Counties seemed unable to satisfy their desire for revenge. There were many ambushes from the Texas side of the river, with the Mexicans trying but failing to retaliate. The Texans carried high-powered rifles that could shoot accurately even at a distance of four hundred yards, so they were safe, and the killings went on for months and months.

It was reported that even Villa petitioned Governor Ferguson of Texas for protection from the terror of hidden ambushers. It was known that Gov. Ferguson gave a Ranger captain the ultimatum of resigning or stopping the violence. Openly, it stopped, but new plans were formulated in secret. Our scouts risked their lives in the bosque and knew what went on, nobody fooled them, and all of us who could not run for the protection of Marfa when trouble started expected retaliation every hour, but not exactly at the time or in the manner in which it came. But somewhere, every man ambushed had relatives and friends who deeply resented his death.

For every Texan ambushed over a six-year period, twenty Mexicans died by ambush, and it is safe to say that over half of this number were innocent victims of the revolution, deprived of their homes and only trying to find a place of safety down the river.

During the period from 1916 to 1921 when I was a soldier and packer in the area, we rode through the bosque with care. The danger led to terror, and the terror led to crimes along the border. But not all of the terror resulted from the actions of outlaws. Some resulted from the actions of the Texas civil authorities.[30]

Chapter 4—The Columbus Raid

When the Columbus, New Mexico, raid took place on March 9, 1916, I was in Troop G of the Eighth U.S. Cavalry stationed at Fort Bliss, at El Paso, Texas. Shortly afterwards, we were ordered to make the trip overland with full pack to the Big Bend to relieve the Sixth Cavalry, which had been there since the area was declared a military district in the previous year.

We moved every bit of equipment and personal property by escort wagons, led all extra horses, ate and slept on the road, and covered twenty-five miles per day, which was good considering the twelve hundred horses involved. Regimental headquarters were at Marfa, Texas.[31] When we reached Valentine, the regiment spent the night there, and in the morning, my troop dropped out and turned south for the forty-mile trip to Evetts Ranch.

First we crossed the twelve-mile flat between Valentine and the beginning of the Viejo Trail at the mouth of Holland Canyon in the Rim Rock. The first mile of the old trail is crooked, rocky, and extremely steep. Although every man and horse made it, it was quite scary to us, as we had never before encountered such a trail.

The heavily loaded pack train preceded us, carrying all of our bags, footlockers, food, and of course oats and baled hay for the horses. It was the most thrilling sight I have ever witnessed. The country from every angle and direction was breathtaking and beautiful. Every time I crossed the Rim Rock in later years, I remembered that first trip.

The trip to Evetts Ranch passed only too quickly. The place was wild and primitive, but there were good quarters for the enlisted men made out of non-creosoted railroad ties from the old abandoned Rio Grande Northern. The cook shack was also made out of railroad ties, and I have never seen better stables and corrals anywhere. The officers' quarters were regulation twelve-foot square field tents with board floors, boarded four feet up all around, each with a wooden door. Water for the camp came from a big spring at the edge of the canyon.

Most of the men we talked to at camp said they had never seen a bandit. They told us that mounted men were constantly moving up and down the San Antone Trail,[32] but they were friendly, and there had never been a shooting incident between Mexicans in Chihuahua and the cavalry in their district. They also said that they had found dead Mexicans who seemed to have been killed from ambush on both of the river trails. The men agreed that violence seemed to coincide with trips to the river by the Texas Rangers.[33]

Twelve miles south of Evetts Ranch on the river was a town called Pilares,[34] and across in Chihuahua was a larger town also called Pilares. Four miles upriver was a town called Porvenir which had its own sister village across the river, and four miles above that was the Upper Nevill Ranch, the last settled place before reaching Bosque Bonito. Downriver from where the trail branched at Pilares, there was only the Sánchez goat ranch occupied by Luis Sánchez, his wife, and family.

Colonel George T. Langhorne was regimental commander. We of the Eighth considered him the finest officer in the entire army. My own troop was commanded by Captain Henry Anderson. Both he and First Lieutenant Christierson were wonderful officers, the kind you would pick to ride the river with. The morning after our arrival, Troop G of the Sixth pulled out with the pack train carrying all of their gear, and we were left on our own to guard fifty miles of the wildest and roughest part of the Big Bend.

I stayed in the Big Bend for almost seven years. Following my first assignment in Troop G, I joined Troop K at the invitation of Captain Leonard F. Matlack. After my discharge, not wishing to leave the river, I stayed for two years and worked on the pack trains.

For years, many people thought the murderous raids, smuggling, and ambushing on the border in the early part of the century were caused by the actions of Mexican revolutionaries. Feelings over the Columbus, New Mexico, raid in 1916 ran high and there was open talk of revenge. Many wild and unsubstantiated rumors contributed to the fear. Typically, the truth of incidents along the river was never documented. For example, in one incident, several witnesses had appeared at the cavalry camps at Indio and Ruidosa and told the captains that three Mexican men had been shot by ambushers in Texas. But when officers, scouts, and men from the cavalry camp had gone to the scene to investigate, they found no evidence of a river crossing. Yet Americans generally believed the men were killed by Mexicans, and also believed, although that belief was disputed by some, that it was Pancho Villa who ordered the raid on Columbus during which sixteen Americans were killed and the town burned down.

Americans also believed that President Carranza of Mexico welcomed American General John J. Pershing, who led the Punitive Expeditionary Forces into Mexico in retaliation for the Columbus raid, and that the First Punitive Expedition was a success. But I was there keeping a careful record, and although Villa's followers were pushed back, Pershing's forces failed, just as Carranza's generals had failed, to capture Villa or even to discourage the revolution.

To those who are determined to believe that Villa was guilty of the Columbus raid, I would ask, "Who saw him?" And who were the white American riders, who outnumbered the

Mexicans, who were there helping? Even now there are men living who can answer that question.[35]

My view is the Columbus raid was a crude Carranzista trap and the raids that followed were made by grieving, outraged relatives trying to avenge the murders of their loved ones, with perhaps some friends who joined them in sympathy. An acquaintance of mine who was a captain on Villa's staff through the terrible years of 1916 and 1917, a man who is today a successful businessman in Nogales, Sonora, swears that he was with Villa in Torreón, six hundred miles to the south, when a Carranza dispatch reached there telling of the Columbus raid. My friend told me that Villa laughed long and loud over the news. Because he loved notoriety, the dispatch was a boost to his ego, so that night he held a great celebration and all of Torreón rang with the cry: "Viva, Villa!"

Furthermore, one of my cousins, who lived in Columbus at the time of the raid, hid to avoid being molested, and from her hiding place plainly saw Americans in the raiding party. Having been raised on the border and knowing Mexicans, she could not have been mistaken. She also overheard a conversation take place between three men talking in English who referred to each other as Lee, Oscar, and Charlie. How many Mexicans bear such names?

Francisco Villa was a crude, uneducated man, unable to read or write. Few of his Mexican followers were educated. He must have been financed by someone who was wealthy, because the poor peons who worshiped him could not have provided him with money. They could rarely afford even a pair of *zapatos* to wear on their feet. In the beginning of his rebellion, Villa knew nothing whatever of military tactics, but he learned fast from American soldiers of fortune. His concept of government was to take from the rich and give to the poor. It is true that he wished to be president of Mexico, and the peons of Mexico followed him blindly. Even today, he is a hero.

Carranza, a highly educated man, realized that if the revolution continued, bandits would soon control his country, and he would be left without credit or respect. Constantly, he reminded his generals by way of stinging dispatches of their responsibility, which Carranza viewed as the extermination of Villa and his army. Considering the tremendous size of Chihuahua alone, with its terrible mountains and bosque, and transportation being what it was in those days, Carranza's army had a job on its hands.

When Carranza took over the country, a third of the regular army was without shoes and many Federal soldiers were clothed in the pantaloons of the Yucatecans and Yaquis. During the four years preceding Carranza's presidency, the soldiers had not known from one day to the next who their commander-in-chief might be. But as the violence progressed, the motivation of the Federal soldiers under Carranza began to build. Now they had an occasional payday, ate regularly, and were issued shoes and ammunition.

★ ★ ★

Downriver from the village of Bosque Bonito was the Upper Nevill Ranch, our headquarters, now known as Green River. It was at that old adobe house that the telephone line from Lobo terminated. The river used to roar louder there behind the old house than at any other place. It makes a sharp turn just where a four-foot ledge of rock runs all the way across, with a deep box canyon just below.

We used to lie prone on that ledge of rock and watch the trail in Chihuahua. Many strange sights passed beneath us. The greatest number of mounted men we saw from the ridge was 120. They were Villa soldiers going downriver toward Ojinaga carrying a black and red flag, or guidon, with the words "Viva Villa" on both sides. The soldiers were very well mounted and heavily armed, and appeared to be well organized and disciplined.

A great many Carranzistas passed up and down the river also, usually in groups of twenty to twenty-five, and almost any day you could see the red flaggers, the "Colorados," deserters from both Villa and Carranza, who would be executed if they were caught. In addition to both revolutionary armies and the Carranzistas, there were the bandits, always ready to join an outfit, run, or fight.

The most pathetic of all river travelers were the family groups trudging along, carrying all of their possessions. Having been left homeless by the revolution, they were trying to find a place of safety for their families. Children of every age were in each group, which also included milk goats, burros, pigs, chickens, and occasionally a cow. The burros were always either ridden or packed, and those that carried packs were always sure to have, at the very top of the load, a well-anchored chicken coop.

Every family member had duties to perform, especially the boys, the least popular task being driving the hogs. They brought up the rear, and it seemed the drivers were always angry at their charges and giving an occasional whack with a stick to a contrary pig. When this happened, the pig would let out a terrible squeal and then go grunting back to the trail. Imagine: the squealing of pigs, the bleating of goats, an occasional bawl from the cow, the constant barking of dogs, and the pitiful crying of small children, most of whom were probably crying from exhaustion or hunger. Some of the processions were comical, but most were pitiful and tragic.

When I returned to the bosque, years later, I climbed the lookout hill, but there was not a living thing to be seen. Everything seemed enveloped in a deep silence, and only by straining my ears could I hear the feeble murmur of the tiny stream of water in the channel that had once contained the mighty Rio Grande. The murmur could have been a funeral dirge for the innocent souls whose blood had soiled its waters and its bosque.

Chapter 5—The Brite Raid

On Christmas Day 1917, quite a number of men from my Troop G were in Valentine, Texas. Just as we were beginning Christmas dinner, the callboy from the Galveston, Houston, and San Antonio Railroad ran in and yelled, "Brite's Ranch is being raided by bandits and there's no one there except the foreman."

Well, that ended our Christmas dinner. Captain Anderson, our troop commander, was there, too, and our only thought was how to get to the ranch quickly. It was about twenty-five miles out, and the dirt road was something to remember. It was only a ranch road and full of ruts. Our horses were in the corral there at Valentine, but it would have been a hard two-hour ride.

In a few moments, the street in front of the drugstore was full of 1915 and 1916 model cars, mostly Oldsmobiles and Hupmobiles. I think twelve cars made the trip, and more than twenty townspeople, all with rifles, went along with the cavalry. All of the cavalry soldiers had rifles with sixty rounds of ammunition, and .45 automatics with twenty-one rounds for the pistols. Roughly, there were thirty cavalrymen, so over fifty armed men piled into those cars, which were touring models for the most part, and tore out toward Brite's Ranch.

Luke Brite, as he was known to us, had one of the finest ranches in Presidio County, situated near the Rim Rock on the dirt road to Candelaria. This road was one of two in over a hundred miles that were suitable for vehicles to cross the Rim Rock to the river. Mr. Brite had quite a few buildings at headquarters, and a large commissary with a post office. Someone from the Valentine outfit seemed to know that the foreman, Van Neill, and his family, including his father Sam, a former Texas Ranger, were all on the ranch, and when that word got around, our anxiety increased. The trip, if made today, would take perhaps twenty-five minutes, but it took us almost an hour over those terrible roads, partly because we had to abandon one car after stopping to repair two flat tires.

A group from Marfa arrived about the same time we did. I think Mr. Brite was there, but I didn't see him. The foreman—who had made a real fight of it, killing one and wounding two—told us the raiders had been gone less than an hour. When we looked with the glasses, we could see dust near the Rim Rock four or five miles away. I'm not exactly sure about distances here, nor do I remember the buildings clearly. It was my first and last time to ever visit Brite's

Ranch, since it was always out of our territory. Protecting it from the Candelaria Road was K Troop's responsibility.

The foreman told us there were about twenty or more bandits, and that they had stolen three horses out of the corral, looted the commissary, and killed the mail carrier, Mickey Welsh.[36] I never learned whether Mickey drove up during the raid or was at the ranch before it started. Anyhow, they hanged the poor old Irishman in the commissary and cut his throat.

We all tore out on the Candelaria road in the direction of the dust, and we could eventually see the men and animals by using glasses. We had to overtake them before they got into the Rim Rock or else lose them, and we had trouble seeing because of the dust, but when we reached a rise of ground, we found they were only a thousand yards in front of us and to the right of the road. The drivers poured it on, but believe me, the bandits were pouring it on, too. I have never seen such whipping and spurring.

They abandoned the pack animals. Although we could see the mules were not too heavily loaded, all of the loads were crooked and about to come off. We almost lost sight of the bandits when one of the cars suddenly stopped and all the others followed suit. I was in the third car behind the leader. We all jumped out and ran to a little ridge, but for a moment the dust was so bad we couldn't see.

During that time we heard the bandits yelling, but not a shot had been fired. Then we could see again, and we fired as rapidly as we could. When the men and their horses started falling, the desperation of those bandits was almost comical. We had been about six hundred yards behind them when the firing started, but now the distance was over a thousand yards, too far for any accuracy at all, even when shooting at a horse. I suppose we cavalrymen killed all of the ones that went down in that wild firing, because although every civilian shot at them as fast as we did, only one man had a rifle capable of shooting effectively that far without a lot of luck. All of their rifles were 30-30 saddle guns, and short ones at that.

It was dangerous work getting up to the bandits on the ground. Two were alive and pinned under their dead horses, and I, for one, was thankful when a civilian from Marfa took care of them. Van Neill, Brite's foreman, had surely shot two of the dead men, for they had crudely bandaged arms. I was surprised at my reaction to all this. It may sound strange, but at the time it seemed perfectly normal to have no feeling whatever, being there among the dead men, or leaving them on the ground with their eyes and mouths open.

We carried all of the loot to the cars from the mules and horses that were knocked down or that we could catch. Two mules were down close to the road ahead of us, so a car went up after their loads. Greediness had been the bandits' downfall; if they had taken only what they could have carried on horseback, they could have escaped.

It was 4:30 p.m. when we returned to the ranch, where horses had materialized from somewhere, and everyone with a saddle in his car soon had a horse ready. One man, already mounted, was thrown hard; that horse didn't know what to make of so many automobiles. Eleven men finally got mounted, all of them civilians, and took after the bandits, even though it seemed their start was too great for the civilians to catch them.

We stayed at the ranch and helped fix Mickey Welsh for the trip to Marfa. The foreman's family was all right. They had been in the house, but the bandits had not rushed the house at all, no doubt because of the attractive loot in the commissary.[37] Fortunately, the telephone wires were not cut. If they had been, the Brite raid would have been a success.

The cowboys returned at dusk, having been unsuccessful at overtaking the bandits. Before we left for Valentine, the foreman and his wife told Captain Anderson there was a girl with the bandit gang, but this information was never verified. If there was a girl riding with the bandits, it would have been the only case I ever heard of. The count when we returned to Valentine that Christmas evening was fifteen dead: one American, Mickey Welsh, one bandit killed by the foreman, and thirteen bandits killed down in the Rim Rock foothills. One thing that seemed strange was all of the raiders I saw that day were middle-aged.

Captain Matlack, with K Troop at Candelaria, took up the trail in Chihuahua early the next morning. Near the river they found a wounded man who was in shock but able to talk. He told Captain Matlack that Placido Villanueva, a small bandit leader who had a hangout below Terlingua, had been the raid's leader, and that he had been shot in the foothills before they reached the Rim Rock Trail. The man also said he had only joined the raiders for food and clothing, which he knew could be found at the Brite commissary.

The wounded raider denied having any cause to harm Mr. Brite or anyone at the ranch. But he also told Captain Matlack that Villanueva's cousin and two friends had been killed by ambush below Terlingua two months earlier, and the raid on Brite's Ranch was planned in revenge. They were only the words of a bandit, but from one who was dying, and whatever the case, it added up to the pattern that followed: kill, kill, ambush, ambush, then more raids.

Fifteen miles below the border, Matlack caught up with and surprised two more bandits, and although some may have escaped by splitting up at the river, that ended the Brite raid, and the lives of eighteen men. Oh, it was a lousy, rotten, ghoulish business, but my feeling was the raid was probably the consequence of ambushes, and the dying bandit was right in saying the raid was planned by the Mexicans for revenge. The avenger lying in ambush had no scruples; he did not care to what degree the repercussions of his terrible acts affected innocent people. My feeling about ambushers has always been that their prospects in the Hereafter will be stark terror.

Chapter 6—Patrolling the Border

The Brite raid forced us to be more intensely alert. The river had to be patrolled, with only the scouts and our patrols available to do it. Every patrol consisted of a non-commissioned officer and four men. Our camp was thirteen miles straight north of Pilares, Texas, a village of twenty houses on the edge of the river. The trail at the edge of the bosque paralleled the river all the way. Two patrols started out at the same time from camp every other day, and when they reached the river, one patrolled to the east as far as the ford below the Sánchez goat ranch, while the other turned upriver through Porvenir to the Upper Nevill Ranch adobe. On their way back, each would contact the incoming patrol.

Government scouts patrolled the entire fifty miles at their discretion. On patrols, I have encountered as many as 250 Mexicans, all of them armed, within pistol range. On many occasions we passed from twenty to fifty armed men and exchanged greetings, and in spite of all the ambushing, never but once during all of our time on the river did Mexicans fire on us, and that was not an ambush. Yet, all of the bandits and killers in the Big Bend were rumored to have been Mexicans.

On the one occasion we were fired upon, we were never sure—since we were not in uniform—if they even knew we were U.S. cavalrymen. There were fifteen Mexicans in the group, and as we had seen them far upriver, we waited for them to pass. As we sat there on our horses on the lip of a sharp bluff, we were actually thirty feet above the bosque. At the point where the bandits had to pass, perhaps five hundred yards separated us, with the bosque and the river in between. The trail there ran through heavy mesquite, and at no time, even using glasses, could we see all of the Mexicans at once.

At a small opening in the brush, they pulled up and looked at us for a while, and then suddenly, without dismounting, they fired at us. About thirty shots were fired while we fell off our horses, but I don't believe their shooting at us did anything except surprise everyone, because—as was always the case—their shooting was poor and all of the shots fell short except one. One might have been a ricochet, for it sang over us like an angry bumblebee, causing all of us to flinch. Falling on our bellies behind the lip of the bluff, we returned their fire, bringing down two horses with the first volley.

There were no open targets in the thick vegetation, but we could hear the yelling that was characteristic of the Mexicans when they were shooting, and they did some wild running to get hidden quickly in the bosque. The binoculars I always carried on the sling strap around my neck, without a case, allowed me to watch the men who could be seen. They had not returned our fire, and after that first volley in which each of us fired a couple of times, we stopped firing.

The two men whose horses were down had crawled away on their bellies. We had been able to see them without glasses as they did so, but now all of them were hidden from our view and we only occasionally saw a part of some horse. We knew they had no chance whatever in a shootout, so we just waited and watched, wondering why they had shot at us in the first place, who they were, and where they were headed.

It was less than an hour until sundown. As I swept the glasses up and down the river, and watched the spot where the horses lay, suddenly I spotted a flash of light from one of the dead horses, which had fallen on its side. On the near side, the sun had broken through, and was reflecting like a mirror from some object. In a few seconds the light changed, and by pulling my horse a little closer, I could see with my glasses that the reflection had bounced off a saber scabbard. Only occasionally had we ever seen anything like a saber, and when we did, it was always on a Carranzista officer. In towns, the shiny saber brought an officer a great deal of attention, but very few were ever carried on the river.

I passed the glasses around so we could all have a good look. The saddle on that horse was another thing besides the saber scabbard that held our attention. It surely looked like a U.S. Cavalry McClellan, and we wondered about that, I can tell you. Both horses could be seen plainly, since the sun was just at the right angle then. The saddle on horse number two was an old big-horned Chihuahua, but that was about all we could determine.

We were afraid the Mexicans intended to wait for darkness before they moved, and also that they might have been the advance guard of a larger group. The man in charge always made the decisions, and in this case, I was the one who was completely responsible. Leaving two men at the spot, I took the other two and made a quick run about a mile up the trail to a high ridge that gave us a good view for three miles upriver. We saw no dust or anything else to indicate a larger group. As we returned downriver, we looked at a ford we had not bothered with on the way up and found signs that a crossing had been made. Both banks were wet, with fresh droppings on our side, but the horses and their riders had not gone over fifty feet from the river into the Texas bosque.

We returned to the other men, who told us nothing had happened while we were gone. It was now almost sundown. Then a half-mile downriver, the group suddenly appeared again, two of them riding double. They were walking the horses and all were looking back, one through a short telescope. As they continued on down the trail, we noticed one thing about them was remarkable: I don't believe any of them was over sixteen years of age, and their actions were childlike.

In the armies of Mexico, it has been estimated that three hundred thousand boys under sixteen years of age served during the Revolution.[38] However, all of the young boys we had ever seen before were in the charge of a veteran officer. This group that we had our little engagement with could have been deserters from Carranza's army or even Villistas, but we never did find out.

The sun was down by then, and we decided to cross the river to the dead horses. Leaving two of our men as lookouts to cover us, and taking only our .45's, we waded across. The river was rather wide at this point, and about hip deep. Crossing it was easy, provided you didn't step in a hole. We crawled up to the first horse, which had been a good one, by his confirmation at least, and sure enough, there was a scabbard with a fine saber in it.

The saddle was a beat-up McClellan with "No. 79, Troop K, 6th U.S. Cavalry" stamped deep into the leather. At that time there was no such thing as war surplus, and just how the saddle came to be in Mexico was anybody's guess. The saber was the most beautiful I have ever seen. I had known many officers who wore sabers while in full dress or on parade, but this one was delicately made, no doubt by some expert in Spain. Both scabbard and saber were silver plated and new. On the hilt, beautifully and artistically engraved, was the name of a lieutenant and some other words in Spanish.

The saddle had been cinched on the horse with an old strap, so after cutting the strap and leaving it under the horse, we carried the saddle and saber to the riverbank and went back to horse number two, which had a big-horned saddle that turned out to be no good at all. But we took the saddlebags with us. In one pocket was a new pair of sergeant's chevrons and a faded paper with some Spanish writing on it. The chevrons were quite large, and black with red stripes. From the stripes hung tassels with small bells at the ends. The only legible word was Roberto. The other pocket contained a small pair of Spanish cavalry spurs.

Taking the saddlebags and their contents, along with the saddle and saber, we waded back across the river. We took the loot on our horses and returned to camp. When I reported the incident to Captain Anderson and turned over the loot we had seized, he reported the happenings to Marfa headquarters, and everybody concerned seemed to agree with us that the incident had been kid's play, considering the way it turned out, and that we had been shot at only to see if we would run. In view of their behavior, we thought the Mexicans might have ventured across to see how it would feel to be on Texas soil.

We went back that night, arriving at the upper place at midnight, and camped. I never learned what became of that beautiful saber after giving it to the captain. I still have the chevrons and spurs. This incident was recorded in Big Bend history, slightly exaggerated. My name was not correctly spelled, and in the written history, the Mexicans who fired on us were identified positively as Federal soldiers. I simply don't know how the writer of that bit of history knew they were Carranza's soldiers, because no one saw them except the five men of our patrol, and even we didn't know. Such insignificant incidents, exaggerated and blown up by writers for over forty years, were eventually described as battles. Everything that happened in the Big Bend seemed always to have been exaggerated.

The Rio Grande was supposed to have run red with blood spilled by thousands of Mexican bandits. Only last month, I read in a magazine of a raid by 360 drunken, screaming Mexican bandits who killed everyone in their path, which extended over sixty miles into the wild Big Bend country of Texas. These bandits were supposed to have shot their victims from horseback at a dead run and then crushed their heads with rifle butts as they rode by. The Texas Rangers supposedly got wind of this orgy of murder, and killed all the bandits they could, and when they ran out of ammunition, chased the others screaming back across the Rio Grande. Stories like that make me boil, and I often wonder if anyone believes them.

Well, my only comment on that story is this: After all that riding and killing, the bandits should have been worn down to a nub, and secondly, their wild mustangs—yes, it was said they rode wild mustangs—after going at a dead run for over a 120 miles, must have been slightly winded when they reached Mexico. Such a fast, long run would, I am sure, have foundered an ordinary horse.

Surely you know how I feel about a good horse, and in that country every man had to rely heavily on his horse. By paying close attention to an intelligent horse, we could avoid ambushers and other dangers. A horse is not only intelligent; he has in his make-up a few other things simply beyond human understanding. Some mysterious sense tells him a great many things that even a good dog would know nothing about. I say this because I have seen dogs trot right over places a horse would pay careful attention to.

On that trail, on both sides of the river, I found spots that were almost impossible to ride over, but not until after the Porvenir massacre did I know the reason. For two years after the massacre, it was not possible to get a horse near the place, and even after twenty years, when I was down there last, the horse I was riding shied away. Surely this proves how supernatural—or whatever you wish to call it—a horse can be.

There are many, many places in the bosque that your horse will shy away from. If you dismount and make an examination, you may find nothing, but you may be sure you are at the scene of some past violence. Certainly a human being was killed there, if not murdered, and even if the horse is hungry, and rich green grass is growing all over the ground, he'll not take one mouthful. A dog may protect you to a degree and warn you of danger, but that same dog can be bribed with a hamburger or even a bone. Just try bribing a horse to ride into a dangerous place, even with sugar or an apple. He will carry you swiftly and safely away from danger, and if the occasion ever demands, he will faithfully give you his life.

Chapter 7—The Spy

Whenever people talk about the law enforcement officers of Texas, especially during the time of the border troubles, what they are referring to is the Texas Rangers. Although they were often involved in the border conflict, the Rangers always got back to safe inland towns in a hurry, and never did they ride the river. The civil officers who ran the risks, who were always on the border during this period, were the scouts, the immigration officers, and the customs men, and the soldiers, mostly cavalrymen, and we certainly knew they were the men who were always facing trouble.

After the Brite raid, a deathly quiet settled over the Big Bend. It was certainly noticeable on the river. No one had a name for it, but it was like the stillness that precedes a cyclone. Troop and bandit movements in Chihuahua were always slow during the cold weather months, but that had nothing to do with the feeling that prevailed down on the border at the time.

We saw a lot of the scouts, who would occasionally spend a night in our camp. The homes of the scouts were their campfires and bedrolls, which they laid out each night in some little draw or canyon, winter and summer, but always near the bosque and the river. Each scout carried a good pair of U.S. Army binoculars, and being on the river all of the time, they were the most well-informed men down there.

The killing of the immigration officers, the Brite raid, and the deadliest part of the reign of terror caused by the ambushing, were all closely connected. At the time, the United States was at war with Germany, of course, and the Germans wanted Mexico to join them in the war, but to our knowledge, no Germans ever tried to cross the river or were seen at any time. Still, it was part of our special orders always to be on the lookout for them, or any suspicious characters, although we were not to arrest them.

One day Drake and his partner, Giles, visited our camp with news: A crossing from Texas into Mexico at the Sánchez ford had been made by a Mexican American who had been back-trailed almost to Marfa. The scouts knew the man had moved into a small jacal in Pilares, Chihuahua, and that he was still there. This incident lent a little more certainty to our feeling that something was in the wind, for sure. How they learned about the man, I can't tell, but the scouts were not guessing when they said, "We don't like it. That man is up to something that's going to spell trouble." It was the opinion of Drake and Giles that the man had been sent by the Rangers.

This called for special work. We watched the spy's jacal day and night. The spy, who was little more than a boy, stayed in Pilares for four days, then left and went straight back to Marfa by the same route that he had traveled going down. During his stay in Pilares, although he never left the vicinity of his jacal, five different men who all seemed friendly, including one who carried a guitar, visited him. None of the men were armed, and all of them were on foot and lived there in Pilares.

The scouts watched the spy from some distance with binoculars after he crossed into Texas, the distance from the river being less than two hundred yards. He didn't carry anything in the way of firearms, and had only the old saddle that he was riding. This is important, because later on, he was reported to have had the saddle, rifle, and six-shooter belonging to one of the immigration officers killed earlier. It was further reported he had found them in the possession of a man in Pilares, and somehow carried them all with him, and that the scouts also knew who the man's companions were when he came into possession of them. When the spy arrived at Marfa, it was reported, he turned the damning physical evidence over to the Rangers.

An important figure in the spy episode was a bandit who lived around San Antonio and Ruidosa, Chihuahua, whom the Rangers had been trying to catch for a long time. This man was Chico Cano, a half-breed native of Texas, who had been accused of stealing T.O. cattle and selling them to willing Texas buyers at $5 per head. With the Rangers after him, he simply crossed the river and was branded a bandit.

Every rancher we talked to about Chico liked him and hoped he wouldn't get caught. He was a good cowboy who had worked all over Jeff Davis and Presidio Counties. Chico was well known to Captain Matlack of K Troop, who had visited with him in Candelaria, eaten with him, and beaten him in a pistol shoot.

Chico had always been reported to be a very fine pistol shot, but still it was expected that Matlack would beat him. I personally believe Matlack was the best shot with a six-shooter who ever lived. He could shoot equally well with either hand, and as he was my troop commander for more than a year, naturally, I knew him very well. Because all of his men considered him the best officer in the Army, his death in 1950 was a sad time for everybody who had ever served under him.

In a few days rumors flew that the Rangers had in their possession the saddle and other equipment taken from one of the immigration officers who had been killed. There were also rumors the Rangers had located this equipment in Pilares and Porvenir. With those rumors, the general accusations against Mexican bandits became specific.

Chapter 8—Porvenir: The Massacre

In February 1918, four heavily armed men rode into our camp. Each was wearing two belts full of shells and two single-action Frontier Model .45 Colts, and on their saddles, in scabbards, they carried Winchesters. None of us had ever seen these men before. They first stopped at Van Evetts' house, which was nearby, and talked to him for a few minutes. We learned that they had come by car from Marfa to the Poole Ranch, where they had horses waiting, and had crossed the Rim Rock to our camp by the Viejo Trail. Van told us later they were drinking, had given him a drink of good whiskey, and had mentioned to him they were after an outlaw.[39]

The strangers inquired as to where Captain Anderson could be found, and when Van pointed out his tent, they mounted again and rode over. The leader got down and called out, and the captain walked over to the men, who introduced themselves and handed him an envelope. Captain Anderson opened the letter and read its contents, glancing at the men, who seemed ill at ease, as he did so. They talked a few moments before going into the Captain's quarters. It was about 4:00 o'clock in the afternoon, and after supper we noticed their horses were still standing beside the tent, saddled and ground hitched.

After we had eaten that night, the captain called all the officers and non-commissioned officers together and said, "The men you see over there are Texas Rangers from Captain Fox's company at Marfa. They are looking for bandits. They brought a letter from their captain, and also a note from Colonel Langhorne. I have talked to him by phone, and this is what we are to do: assist them in any way they desire, and the first and, I believe, the only way they will need us, so they tell me, is to surround and search the village of Porvenir. They tell me they want to make certain that all weapons are seized and that no one escapes."

Then Captain Anderson continued. "The Colonel feels that we have to help them, but personally, I don't like what I have to do. This is the oddest request that I've ever heard of and I hope everything turns out all right. These men don't even know where the village is located. They have told me the principal reason for their being here is to capture Chico Cano, and that they know he will be there tonight. The part about leaving at midnight sounds screwy to me. They say they also want to catch a couple more bandits."

Then he turned to First Sergeant Dingman and said, "Have forty volunteers ready to leave here at 10:30 p.m." He waited for a while and then laughed as he said, "The business doesn't seem right to me at all, but the people at headquarters seem to think that it is not unusual and that these men, being Rangers, surely know their business."

But he added, "I don't like it—and the idea of them thinking that Porvenir is armed really is amusing. If we find a butcher knife down there, it will be a surprise to me. Have any of you ever seen Chico Cano?" he asked. None of us had, so that was ended.

We were shocked, since some of us had spent an hour that very afternoon visiting at Porvenir. We had bought six dozen eggs for the mess sergeant, which was normal procedure for all home-coming patrols. We knew the people living in Porvenir better than I know my next door neighbor today, and we were sure they wouldn't harbor outlaws, and that Chico Cano was as unfamiliar to them as he was to us.

It was not unusual for the Rangers to ask for assistance from the cavalry troops, and for the cavalry to oblige. Yet, the more we kicked the strange request around, the more certain we felt that something was seriously wrong. Sergeant Simpson and I had made a full report to First Sergeant Dingman when our patrols arrived. By mutual consent, we both went directly to Captain Anderson, as we never needed permission to talk to him. We told him how we felt about the Rangers' request.

The captain agreed with us, saying he had vigorously protested to Colonel Langhorne that we were sure there weren't any outlaws in Porvenir, but the Colonel had insisted there was nothing wrong with helping the Rangers.

As we were leaving the captain's tent, he said, "I feel pretty strongly about this, but we will keep our eyes open, and try to learn what they are really up to. They won't find Chico Cano in Porvenir tonight, so we don't have anything to worry about. There isn't any doubt in my mind that these men are not as brave as they pretend to be, because they asked me if I was certain that I could guarantee protection.

"They also asked how many men were in Porvenir. I told them we had never counted noses, but it was usually seven or eight and sometimes twelve because they worked all over the country. They tried to make me believe the men were all bandits, but I offered to make them a wager that we wouldn't find a firearm in the village."

After leaving the captain's tent, the Rangers walked over to their horses, built a small fire, and hunkered around it. We couldn't help but notice that not one of them thought to loosen the cinches on their mounts. A few of our men walked over to the fire to admire the horses and got a cool reception.

When our men returned, one remarked, "I don't know what they are up to, but I never saw four men act so tough and look so scared."

⭑ ⭑ ⭑

It was a bitterly cold night, and although it was quite dark when we set out, there would later be a moon. It was the seventh year of the revolution, and Porvenir had a clean record, although it was at the southwestern tip of Presidio County. How could they be harboring the Big Bend's most famous bandit? Not once had any of them caused us any trouble whatever. They were all good Mexicans.

When we reached Porvenir at midnight, we had to work fast for several reasons. One was the intense cold. Another was to see that no one slithered away. None of us expected to see any outlaws in that friendly place. These people were our friends. They had ridden to our camp one night to report a large group of mounted men in Chihuahua, because they knew we would want to observe their actions.

Working quickly, we surrounded the small village before a single dog barked, or a light showed. All of the families lived in mud and pole jacales except two, whose two-room adobes had the only glass windows in the village.

Routing an entire village out of their warm beds at midnight in freezing weather wasn't a pleasant task. Most of the able-bodied men were away that night, which was not unusual because they worked all over Marfa, Alpine, Valentine, and Van Horn, and in both counties on ranches whenever they could. But the river was home to them, and they had been there for years. Every family had a garden, some had milk cows, and a few raised goats and chickens. We bought all of their surplus produce, which pleased them.

A few of the villagers spoke English, and one girl—a young mother with a two-year-old boy—was our interpreter whenever we needed one. She had attended school in Valentine, and her father worked for the Means Ranch in the Davis Mountains.

We tried to be civil and decent as we went through the village in the dark, arousing the people out of their humble homes. We told them they should not be alarmed; it was only a check by some Rangers who were after a bandit. We had heard of such illegal searches before, when Rangers had asked troops to assist them further down the river, and no real harm had been done then.

Overall, the Rangers brought honor to the law enforcement profession. Men of the stature of Frank Jones, James B. Gillett, John Reynolds Hughes, John Coffee Hays, and Leander H. McNelly were men of tact and bravery and an honor to the state. Had they been on the river then, it would never have been necessary to declare the area a military district. But these men were feared. When they were on the river, the word "Rangers" inspired terror, and this story will prove, I believe, that the terror was more than justified. The people of Porvenir insisted there was no stranger there, and hadn't been for weeks. We believed this. We could almost vouch for it ourselves, because we knew what went on down there.

Fifty feet from the village on the east side was a rock bluff about five feet high that ran from the river trail all the way to the riverbank. Over near the bluff, the Rangers stood with their horses while the search went on. After everyone was up and dressed, we got them out into the little cleared place—or compound, as it was called—and someone started a fire.

The only weapons we found were an old single-barreled 10-gauge shotgun with no shells, and a few butcher knives, which we turned over to the first sergeant, who told the captain that we had the weapons and that no one had tried to escape. He, in turn, went over and told the Rangers we had done what they had requested.

"Thank you, Captain," said the leader. "Now we want to question these people. Will you withdraw your men so we can talk to them alone? We will be through here in a few minutes."

The captain replied, "All right, but I don't see anyone who looks like a bandit. They're all old men and boys, and my men know most of them."

Until then, the Rangers had not seen the people of the village close up at all, and for a second nothing was said. But in a moment the Ranger said, "We'll see about that."

We started for the river trail where we had left our horses with the men on detail while the Rangers, leaving their horses and hitching their gun belts, walked over toward the villagers. I doubt if anyone counted the people present that night, but we all agreed later there must have been about thirty-one, including the baby.

What we saw of the four Rangers present that cold February night would have been a shock to any present-day television audience. They didn't act brave. I suppose they were drinking to give themselves courage, because each one acted like the very Devil was chasing him.

No one suspected what was about to happen, and although we did have what you might call a premonition, and smelled some kind of treachery, even the poor, shivering people of Porvenir had no thoughts of murder.

Then, about the time we reached the horses, three hundred yards away, we heard voices, all in Mexican. At first they were men's voices, and they all sounded alike. Then a woman spoke out and another one screamed. Then there was more loud talking, setting our nerves on edge as we strained our ears for the next sound.

Some of the men wanted to go back at once, but our captain said, "Now hold it, boys. Whatever is happening down there doesn't please me any more than it does you, but those men are Rangers—they showed me their warrants of office. Anyone can wear a badge, but these men have warrants from the State, and even if they are full of whiskey, surely they know what they are doing."

For perhaps ten seconds we couldn't hear anything, and then it seemed that every woman down there screamed at the same time. It was an awful thing to hear in the dead of night. We could also hear what sounded like praying, and, of course, the small children were screaming with fright. Then we heard shots, rapid shots, echoing and blending in the dark.

At the first shot, the captain yelled, "Come on, boys!" and we raced toward the compound. As we neared it, we could make out by the reflection of the fire the wild confusion as the Rangers fought to catch their horses. As we were running toward them, when they were mounted, they yelled, "We got him, Captain, we got him," and then, lashing and spurring their horses in every direction, they tore out of there. We could hear them yelling for a long time as they fled down the edge of the bosque.

We were caught in an unexpected and terrifying situation. Hysterical women were all around us, screaming and praying at the same time and pointing toward the bluff. We had a few flashlights, so we threw the beams toward the place where they were pointing. At the foot of the bluff we could see a mass of bodies, but not a single movement. The bodies lay in every conceivable position, including one that seemed to be sitting against the rock wall.

As soon as we were close, we smelled the nauseating sweetish smell of blood, and when we could see, we saw the most hellish sight that any of us had ever witnessed. It reminded me of a slaughterhouse. A hospital corpsman who was with us went over the bodies, but not a breath of life was left in a single one. The professionals had done their work well.

The women crowded closer and our interpreter, who had her little boy in her arms, began to cry out what had happened. She told us they had first tied all the men together with a rope, then hit one with a pistol, knocking him down. They kicked and shoved them over to the bluff, and when she—the interpreter indicated another woman—tried to protest, she, too, was knocked down by the men.

Then the interpreter corrected herself. "No! Not men—beasts, criminals! They had questioned no one at all," she said, "and their first words were threats, but when they were shooting the men, they asked each one, sneering, 'Are you Chico Cano?'

"Thank God," she said, "my husband wasn't here. He's working in Marfa."

Our captain was shocked. "I want all of you to understand," he began, "that we knew nothing of what was going to happen. If we had, we would have stopped them. The men who did this are the law in Texas, but I promise that I will do everything in my power to see that this is properly reported and these men punished."

"Will you please send someone for the Priest?" a woman asked.

"Where is he?" the captain inquired.

"Candelaria."

So a sergeant and three men rode off at once for the priest, twenty miles away.

"I will leave a detail of men here to guard you tonight," the captain said, "and in the morning another detail will be down to help you bury your dead. I will send you food, too, and we will help in any way that we can. You have been good people, and I am badly hurt over what has happened here."

All of the time the women were telling us what had taken place, we were staring at those corpses. Seven murders—or butcherings, they could be called—had been committed in thirty seconds by Texas law enforcement officers. The horribly mangled bodies were a sight that would make any decent person sick. It was one of the blackest pages of Texas history.

The women told us they had been made to face the bluff and then at three feet, with dumdum .45's, the officers had blown seven innocent human beings to pieces. One of the boy's arms was five feet from his body. Another arm hung by a thread of flesh. An old man's entire face was blown away, and the rock bluff was smeared with blood and human tissue. Intestines protruded from every corpse, and the awful stench of blood and bowels hung in the air. The women told us that after all of the men had fallen, the officers had emptied their guns into the bodies on the ground, and when we looked later on, we recovered several of the dumdum slugs.

A screaming, wailing old woman told the captain through the interpreter that the two smaller Rangers had murdered her husband six months before, near Ruidosa. From the survivors we learned the names and ages of the victims, and one of the officers wrote them down. There were two men who were past sixty-five; one about fifty who was small, and had some kind of stomach trouble that prevented him from working; two young men, aged twenty-one and twenty-three; and two boys, one aged fourteen and the other, the youngest of the group, only twelve.

No decent Texan, then or since, would have condoned that awful slaughter. The terrible hatred a few Texans have for Mexicans, a distaste that seems to have sprung up during the past century, would have been hard to understand then. Almost every name in early Texas history, certainly most of the very greatest in legend, song, and verse, were friendly with all Mexicans except Santa Anna and his army, and many were married to Mexican women.[40]

Killing a bandit or even ambushing was common during this time, but enlisting a ring of cavalry protection for wholesale murder was something that had never happened before. The events of that night had a deep effect on every person present, and I believe most of us carried away a pain over our eyes and in our hearts that has never completely gone away.

★ ★ ★

The captain left a detail of ten men with the victims and survivors, promising to carry out his pledge to the poor bewildered people. He was a deeply religious man and felt, as we all did, we had been lied to and used, to protect the people who were the real criminals. It was a sad, quiet trip back to camp, with all of us deep in thought. It would not be difficult to imagine what we were thinking, with the assassins riding wildly somewhere in the night.

It was 4:00 a.m. when we arrived back at camp. A sergeant and six men were asked to get a pack mule, food, blankets, bed ticks, picks, and shovels, and return to Porvenir to assist in the burial of the seven victims. I volunteered for the assignment. But when we arrived after daylight, we found the bodies had been removed across the Rio Grande.

"All of the people left here shortly after you did," the sergeant in charge told us. "They were afraid to stay, and we didn't blame them. They told us they had relatives in Porvenir, Chihuahua,[41] and said they would return in the daylight when the priest arrived.

"About an hour ago an old woman who was here when it happened drove across at the ford in a wagon. She asked us to load the bodies into the wagon, explaining they wanted to hold the burials in Mexico. She also said they wished to bury their own dead. I couldn't see anything wrong with her wishes, so I did what she asked, but I tell you, it was a job that I never want any part of again. One of our men is still sick down there by the river. We only had our hands to work with, you know, and it was a terrible mess.

"Before the old woman brought the wagon over, two Mexicans rode up from Pilares, acting wild. They sat on their horses and stared at the bodies and then one of them dismounted, removed his hat, crossed himself, and got down on his knees and sobbed.

"He pointed to one of the old men, and said, 'That was my father.' He stayed kneeling for a few minutes and then mounted his horse and both of them crossed the river again.

"After the wagon was finally loaded with its awful cargo," he continued, "we saw the boys coming up the trail with the priest, and he just crossed over a few minutes ahead of you." One of our soldiers said, "I don't like this situation; they are bound to be planning revenge over there. What do you think?"

Well, what would anybody think? Our troop was on the river for more than a year after the massacre, and in all of that time the Rangers strutted the streets of inland towns, but not one of them rode the river. Perhaps they knew no cavalry troop would ever protect them in anything again.

As can well be imagined, Porvenir and Pilares, Texas, were deserted after that. Gardens and crops were left neglected and soon died. Both places felt like a graveyard, and any man who was human felt sorry for the people who had, for no reason, been forced to flee their homes.

There were no burials across the river until the evening of the second day, and although it was cold, decomposition must have been far advanced before the bodies were buried. The cavalrymen stood and watched the burials with glasses from across the river.

During all of the time between the killings and the burials, Mexicans were riding in. One group of over a hundred rode in on the second day, but they looked like Villistas, from their equipment and dress, and they moved on before the burials took place.

For days after the massacre, the Mexican men looked and talked angry, and we knew they were planning revenge. Drake and his partner, Giles, the two scouts, were as burned up over the Porvenir mess as we were, and they were in our camp every night the week of the killings, giving us information that a raid was being planned. After that night, everyone on the border began to wonder when the next raid would be pulled off. Rotten as he had been at one time in his life, Drake said, he didn't have anything but contempt for men who could commit the crimes they should be preventing.

Then, one morning, Sánchez and his wife rode into camp at Evetts Ranch and told us they had come to tell us good-bye. They told Captain Anderson they had been warned to get out and that they couldn't risk staying. This came as a great shock to all of us. There wasn't an officer on the river or one who had ever ridden through there who hadn't eaten at the Sánchez table. Their hospitality was known up and down the river. No one was ever turned away, and every rider's horse was given hay and grain. We often wondered: if their place had been the only source of free meals on the river, would they have been given the ultimatum?

Captain Anderson offered them protection, but they declined the offer. When they left, after bidding everyone of us good-bye, there wasn't a dry eye in camp and the Sánchez couple cried openly. None of us ever saw them again.

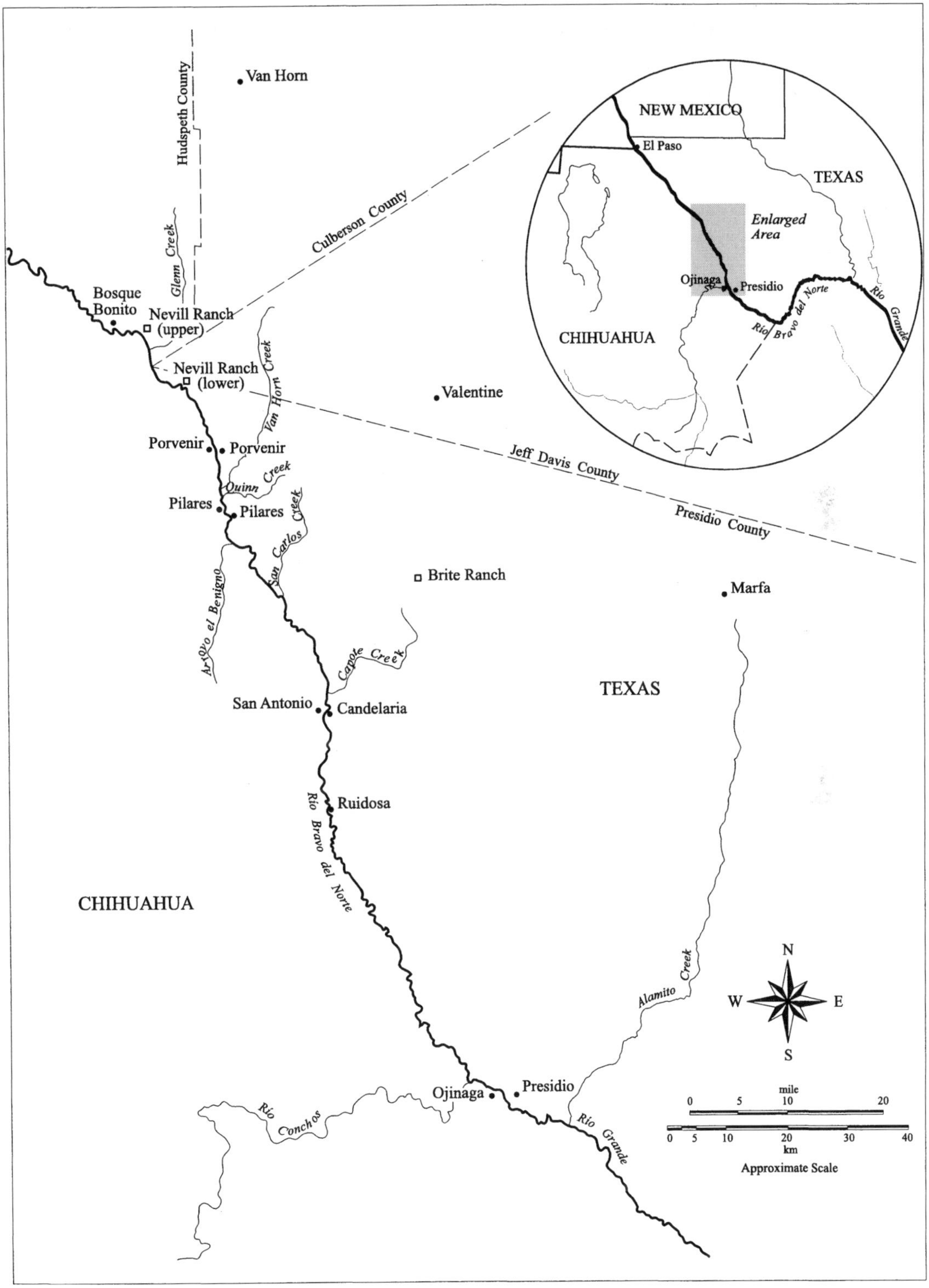
NEW MEXICO
El Paso
TEXAS
Enlarged Area
Ojinaga
Presidio
CHIHUAHUA
Río Bravo del Norte
Río Grande
Van Horn
Hudspeth County
Culberson County
Glenn Creek
Bosque Bonito
Nevill Ranch (upper)
Nevill Ranch (lower)
Van Horn Creek
Valentine
Porvenir
Porvenir
Quinn Creek
Pilares
Pilares
Jeff Davis County
Presidio County
San Carlos Creek
Arroyo el Benigno
Brite Ranch
Marfa
Capote Creek
San Antonio
Candelaria
TEXAS
Ruidosa
Río Bravo del Norte
CHIHUAHUA
Alamito Creek
N
W
E
S
mile
0 5 10 20
0 5 10 20 30 40
km
Approximate Scale
Ojinaga
Presidio
Río Conchos
Río Grande

Christmas at Fort Bliss, 1916. From left around table: Dingman 1st Sergeant, Heimbuch, Hawke, Simpson, Loughman, Rice, Zink, Burns, Shoemaker, Burton, Keil, Nichols, (Standing), Carney, Iddings. The Non-commissioned Officers of Troop G Eighth U.S. Cavalry: Colonel George T. Langhorne, Commanding; Captain Henry H. Anderson, Troop Commander.

ARCHIVES OF THE BIG BEND, BRYAN WILDENTHAL LIBRARY, SUL ROSS STATE UNIVERSITY, ALPINE, TEXAS

ARCHIVES OF THE BIG BEND, BRYAN WILDENTHAL LIBRARY, SUL ROSS STATE UNIVERSITY, ALPINE, TEXAS

Keil and patrol on a ridge overlooking the Rio Grande and Chihuahua, 1918.

The lonely and deserted ranch where Van Evetts lived with his wife and daughter. It was from this outfit that Evetts Ranch cavalry camp got its name. This was all that was left of the camp in 1930.

ARCHIVES OF THE BIG BEND, BRYAN WILDENTHAL LIBRARY, SUL ROSS STATE UNIVERSITY, ALPINE, TEXAS

ARCHIVES OF THE BIG BEND, BRYAN WILDENTHAL LIBRARY, SUL ROSS STATE UNIVERSITY, ALPINE, TEXAS

Cavalry stables, blacksmith and wagon shop at the camp at Evetts Ranch, 1917.

Troopers of Troop K with (second from left) Cavalry Scouts Miles Scannel (Troop K Cavalry 1918–1919) and (second from right) William T. Garlick of Troop G, Eighth Cavalry. Garlick and Scannel were both ambushed and killed later, supposedly by Mexicans from across the river.

PHOTOGRAPHY COLLECTION, HARRY RANSOM RESEARCH CENTER, THE UNIVERSITY OF TEXAS AT AUSTIN

Troop K, Eighth Cavalry, 1917. Candelaria, Texas, Marfa Sector.

ARCHIVES OF THE BIG BEND, BRYAN WILDENTHAL LIBRARY, SUL ROSS STATE UNIVERSITY, ALPINE, TEXAS

Old cottonwood log house at Nevill Ranch. It was here that Glenn Nevill and Rosa Castillo were killed during the last bandit raid in the Big Bend on March 26, 1918.

ARCHIVES OF THE BIG BEND, BRYAN WILDENTHAL LIBRARY, SUL ROSS STATE UNIVERSITY, ALPINE, TEXAS

ARCHIVES OF THE BIG BEND, BRYAN WILDENTHAL LIBRARY, SUL ROSS STATE UNIVERSITY, ALPINE, TEXAS

Glenn Nevill (forefront on horse), Ed Nevill (to the right of Glenn), and some Mexicans from Porvenir, three miles down the river. Mr. Nevill said after the raid that he recognized two of the men the evening of the raid.

Glenn Nevill when he was 14.

ARCHIVES OF THE BIG BEND, BRYAN WILDENTHAL LIBRARY, SUL ROSS STATE UNIVERSITY, ALPINE, TEXAS

Mr. Ed Nevill on Charlie, one of his favorite saddle horses, shortly before his outfit was raided by Mexican bandits on March 26, 1918.

PHOTOGRAPHY COLLECTION, HARRY RANSOM RESEARCH CENTER, THE UNIVERSITY OF TEXAS AT AUSTIN

Left to right, Major Considine, Chico Cano, and Captain Leonard F. Matlack. Chico Cano was considered the Big Bend's most noted bandit.

PHOTOGRAPHY COLLECTION, HARRY RANSOM RESEARCH CENTER, THE UNIVERSITY OF TEXAS AT AUSTIN

Captain Leonard F. Matlack on old Red at Candelaria with a squad of Troop K Cavalry, 1919.

Detailed drawing of how a diamond hitch is formed.

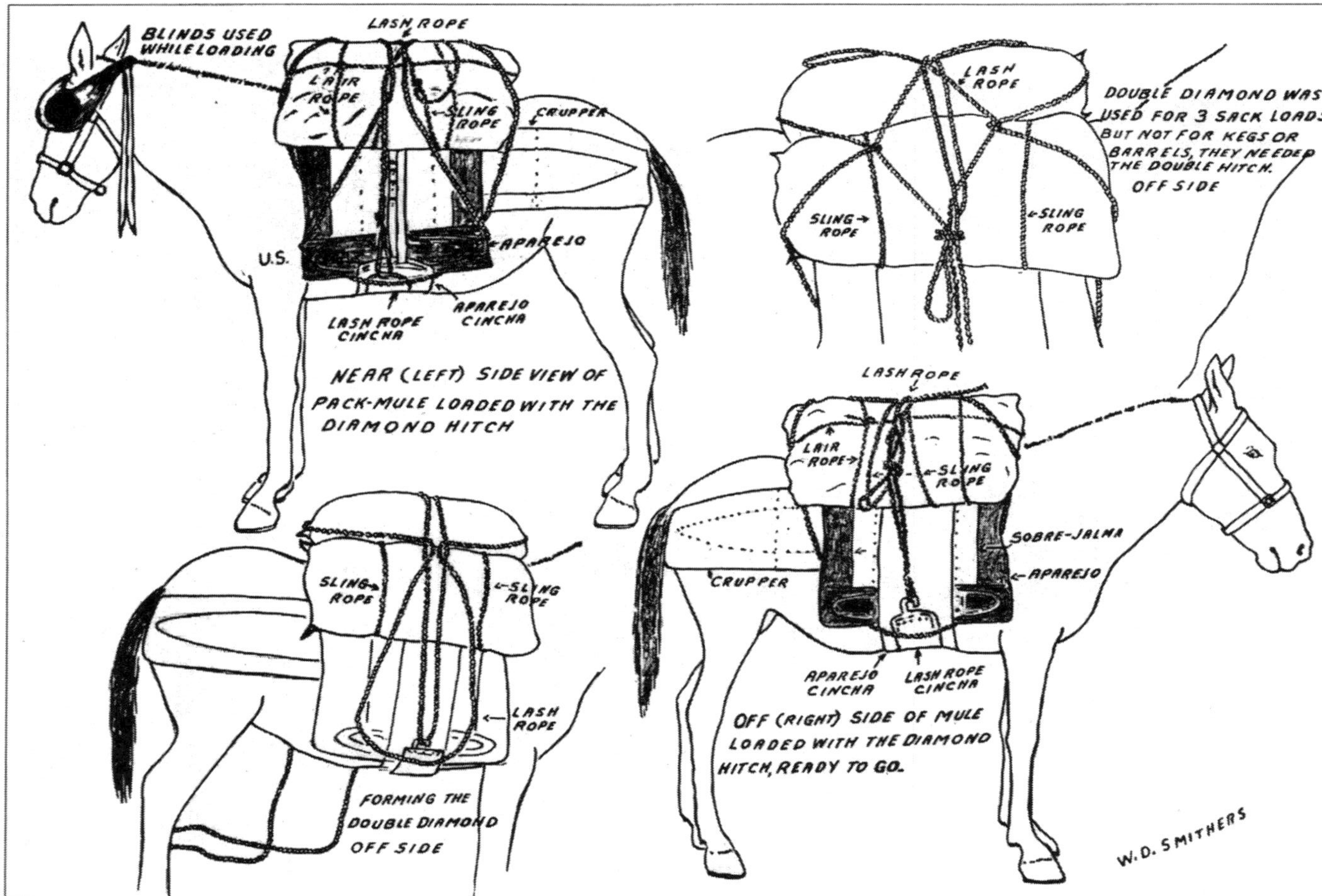

PHOTOGRAPHY COLLECTION, HARRY RANSOM RESEARCH CENTER, THE UNIVERSITY OF TEXAS AT AUSTIN

PHOTOGRAPHY COLLECTION, HARRY RANSOM RESEARCH CENTER, THE UNIVERSITY OF TEXAS AT AUSTIN

Pack train 6 at Candelaria, Texas, in 1917. All fifty mules were loaded with cargos of hay, oats, and supplies for troopers of an outpost at Evetts' Ranch, about forty miles from Candelaria. This train's start was delayed so pictures could be taken. Usually pack trains were well on their way before sunup.

Pack train 6 was strung out as a pack train should be when it was traveling. This picture was taken in 1918 when the train was a mile from Candelaria, Texas, on the road to Pilares and Evetts Ranch cavalry outpost. This road, or trail, was often called the Comedor Trail. This picture shows the entire train spaced out, the packmaster and cook leading, then ten peak mules, two packers, ten more mules, etc.

PHOTOGRAPHY COLLECTION, HARRY RANSOM RESEARCH CENTER, THE UNIVERSITY OF TEXAS AT AUSTIN

Packmaster George Hickle, pack train 6 at Candelaria, Texas, in 1917 or 1918. All fifty mules are lined up behind their aparejos and the ten packers are at the left. The man with the dog was the cargador; the blacksmith and cook are not pictured.

The army camp at Holland Ranch was sixteen miles southwest of Valentine, Texas, and twenty miles east of the Rio Grande. This picture of Camp Holland taken in 1919 shows the trail on the mountain that the pack trains used to reach the camp that was inside Viejo Pass.

PHOTOGRAPHY COLLECTION, HARRY RANSOM RESEARCH CENTER, THE UNIVERSITY OF TEXAS AT AUSTIN

PHOTOGRAPHY COLLECTION, HARRY RANSOM RESEARCH CENTER, THE UNIVERSITY OF TEXAS AT AUSTIN

Pack train 2 arriving at Holland's Ranch in Viejo Pass. The cargo may have been for the cavalry troop that was stationed there or, after an overnight stop, the train may have taken its cargo to Evetts Ranch troop. This picture was taken in 1919 or 1920. Charlie Coward was packmaster and Jeff Davis was the cargedor *then.*

PHOTOGRAPHY COLLECTION, HARRY RANSOM RESEARCH CENTER, THE UNIVERSITY OF TEXAS AT AUSTIN

Pactktrain and troop of cavalry Marfa, Texas, 1918. Camp D. A. Russell in background.

Chapter 9—The Nevill Raid

Captain Anderson's report was such a shock to the high command that they could hardly believe what had really happened. Apparently many hot words and letters were exchanged, reaching all the way to Austin. The captain had the names of the Rangers, but the cavalry soldiers never knew who they were. Two of them resigned, we understood, and the other two left the state.

I was worried about Mr. Nevill, at the Nevill Ranch, and tried to make him realize the position he was in, but he couldn't be made to see any danger. The Mexicans had never bothered him, and the patrols went by frequently. All patrols had a sergeant in charge and usually five men, and each patrol stayed out four days unless something out of the ordinary happened. No matter what did happen, there were always ten men on the river, and except on very rare occasions, no patrol left camp until properly relieved.

The Nevill Ranch was the only American outfit in all of our fifty-mile territory, so it is easy to understand our feelings for them, and when the Nevills were thought of, the Castillos, the ranch foreman and his family who worked for them, were thought of with equal respect.[42] Also, Glenn Nevill, the oldest son,[43] was a close friend during my time there. We had the same interests and spent a lot of time together. Seeing any one of them was always a delight, and certainly some of us saw them every single day. Each patrol stopped by the Nevill Ranch no matter which way they were going, since our outpost camp was at an old adobe eleven miles upriver, known as the Upper Nevill Ranch.

At the Upper Nevill, there was a stout pole corral and a windmill. This camp was four hundred yards from the river, at a point where, in the river, there was as close to a waterfall as at any other place I know of. The shelf of solid rock that cut across the riverbed created a five-foot boiling spillway which really roared when the river was high. It could always be heard but at night the noise in that rocky place seemed to be magnified.

Our telephone hookup with the outside world was located there, the line running to Lobo and the railroad, then from the railroad to Valentine, and from Valentine to Evetts Ranch. The upper adobe was twenty-eight miles from our main camp. The other end of our district was ten miles west of Candelaria, and about the same distance from our headquarters.

Mr. Ed Nevill, a former Texas Ranger,[44] and his son Glenn had their home at the Lower Nevill Ranch, right on the edge of the river not forty miles inland. Mrs. Nevill and the other children lived in Van Horn thirty-five miles away so the children could attend school. The Nevill headquarters house consisted of two large rooms, fourteen by eighteen feet, with good fireplaces, connected by a fourteen-foot screened porch. The roof and all the sheds were made of galvanized iron. The house, however, was built out of six-by-eight-inch railroad ties seven feet in length, as most houses were between the river and the Rim Rock. Mr. Nevill and Glenn lived in the south room. The Castillo family who worked for Mr. Nevill lived in the north room.

Ramón and Rosa Castillo were very good, reliable people who had three children, including a little curly-headed boy of four named José. The other, younger children lived most of their time with their grandmother in Van Horn. Rosa had a crinkly-eyed bubbling personality. She always seemed ready to burst into laughter and usually did so. The little boy was her exact image and had the same friendly, laughing disposition. Rosa, who had been raised in Valentine, was the sister of Maggie Calanche, well known through the Big Bend as a great roper and bronco rider. Ramón was a general handyman who was good at all kinds of ranch work. He was a quiet, serious man about thirty-five years of age.

To the Nevills, Ramón, Rosa, and the little boy were much more than hired hands. They were treated as family, and Mr. Nevill trusted them completely. They had worked for him ever since he had started on the river. At the ranch, Rosa did all the housework and cooked for the five of them, and on many occasions, we ate there too. We always headed for there when we killed a mess of quail, as she had a Dutch oven that would quickly french-fry twenty birds at a time. It was no trouble whatever to kill that many from horseback, so we ate quail all of the time we were down there, winter and summer. The big screened porch served as a dining room in good weather and was also a store room for everything from chicken feed to harnesses.

Everything was kept on the porch except the saddles, which were always left at the shed in the horse corral. From the east, or downriver, side of the porch you could see the river and the trails on both sides. On the west side, you could see the sheds, corral, watering gap, and the river ford. The water gap was a fenced lane from the corral that extended out into the river about ten feet. Every watering place on the ranch was a water gap. Where the banks sloped gently, Nevill had built a fence out about ten feet into the river, then run it parallel to the river bank about fifty or sixty feet and then back to the bank again.

All stock and humans, too, used the watering gaps, and although Mr. Nevill's two thousand cattle ranched all over three hundred square miles, they were never much trouble because they were all forced to water at the river. At the ranch house, Mr. Nevill had a cistern for drinking and cooking water, but he used river water also. We had developed a good spring at our headquarters, but there were only three such springs in the whole country, the best of which, Viejo Spring, was at Lee Means' ranch on the Viejo Trail high in the Rim Rock.

There was lots of shade on the river. There were cottonwood trees and, of course, mesquite and catclaw grew as thick as the hair on a dog's back. Mr. Nevill and Glenn rode the river every day, rain or shine, and whenever possible went along with the patrols. Mr. Nevill was a serious, trail-wise veteran about fifty years of age then. Glenn was my age, and although Mr. Nevill seldom laughed, we had lots of good times together, and all of us learned a lot from Mr. Nevill, who could tell at a glance whether anyone or anything had forded the river. He was infallible when it came to tracks. With only a glance, he could tell whether stock were moving on their own or were being driven. This sounds simple, but it is not.

Both the Nevills and Ramón owned .250-3000 caliber Savage rifles. The Nevills rode fine horses and had two each which they valued more highly than any of the others. These four horses were all dun in color, with black manes and tails and a wide black stripe from the withers to the tail. They were fast, sure-footed and were not gun-shy. You could shoot from their backs and all they would ever move was their ears. All four traveled at a running walk that would keep a good cavalry horse trotting.

The main ranch house, corrals, sheds, and outbuildings were enclosed in a fenced trap with mesquite posts and a four-strand barbed wire fence. It took in a section of land and was used for a horse trap and to restrain any animal that needed to be doctored. The work mules and the milk cow were kept there, and of all the gates in the whole country, the wire gates into Mr. Nevill's horse trap were the only ones to open and close.

★ ★ ★

On March 25, 1918, Mr. Nevill left the ranch at sunup for Van Horn, thirty-five miles away, on business and to see the family. Before he left, he told Glenn, "Son, I want you and Ramón to ride that river all the way, regardless of the patrol. Cut sign[45] at all the fords and keep a sharp look out. You know what happened down the river. I don't believe it will happen to us, but I surely don't want to be gone if it ever does happen. I'll be back the evening of the twenty-sixth," he said and rode off, waving to the little boy, who was up and expected it.

Glenn and Ramón did not ride the river that day. Ramón said later that Glenn got to fooling with a young horse he was breaking, and by the time Ramón reminded him of the river it was too late to start. But on the twenty-sixth they did ride it all the way. Everyone, even newcomers, stayed alert when they rode the river, and with Mr. Nevill gone, there's no doubt Glenn and Ramón were alert when they were on the trail. The horses they rode were so sensitive they never missed anything with their intelligent ears, and would alert a sleeping man at the sound of a covey of quail or a rabbit.

The great mystery is how they missed the raiders, seventeen horses and men, who were in the bosque only four hundred yards away when Glenn and Ramón unsaddled that evening. Mr. Nevill, had he been there, probably would have caught the signs, but Ramón and Glenn did not.

We learned later that the raid on Nevill's ranch was planned in revenge during the burials at Porvenir, and when the patrol passed on the twenty-sixth, the raiders may have been hidden in some brushy draw or could even have been in Pilares.[46] The patrol stopped at the ranch and talked to Rosa about 4:00 p.m. while Glenn and Ramón were on the river and then went on to the Upper Ranch and camped. Before sundown, they saw Mr. Nevill pass by on the trail. He was riding at a fast lope and didn't stop, but waved his hat and the patrol waved back. Soon he disappeared down the trail.

It was just about sundown when he rode into the corral, glad to be back. He unsaddled Charley at the shed and turned him into the trap. Charley was his favorite horse, the largest of the dun-colored saddle horses, while Glenn's Shorty was the smallest of all the saddle stock, although he probably weighed nine hundred pounds. Mr. Nevill even remembered later that Charley rolled and shook himself when he was turned loose in the corral. Picking up his rifle, which he had leaned against the shed, Mr. Nevill started up to the house just as Glenn and the Castillos, who had been eating, came out on the porch.

I hadn't thought Mr. Nevill ever relaxed his constant vigilance, but this night the bandits fooled not only Glenn and Ramón, but also, Mr. Nevill and his horse. This mystery was never explained. It often happened that men have overlooked or failed to detect signs that cost them their lives, but a good horse is infallible. It has always been the opinion of those of us who knew the country and circumstances that the horses did give warning, and in this instance, Mr. Nevill in particular—being tired—simply overlooked it.

His words of greeting were, "Son, did you ride that river?"

"Yes, we did, Dad," Glenn replied.

"See any sign?"

"Not a thing," Glenn answered.

Mr. Nevill relaxed as he greeted Rosa and the little boy, giving each of them a sack of candy. Next he leaned his rifle against the wall with the others and bent to unsnap his chaps. Just then Charley whinnied and they all looked up and saw the river full of Mexican horsemen, about twenty of them, less than four hundred yards away.

The Mexicans began to yell and shoot, riding toward the house. It was dusk by then, and there was wild confusion in the river as the bandits spurred their horses across, throwing water high in the air. Mr. Nevill told us later, "After looking for ambushers and bandits all my life, I simply froze. I saw at a glance there were about twenty of them, and I stood there like a crazy man and counted them—yes, I did—and there were seventeen men." Those were his exact words.

Physical evidence later on verified that count, and the last time I talked to Mr. Nevill at his Midday Cafe in Alpine, Texas, in September 1934, he told me over and over, "Yes, sir, Bobby, there were seventeen of them," and then for the very first time he told me something else. "I recognized Juan and Julio Mendoza. They lived at Porvenir and had worked for me several times and were good men." He was still planning to go back to the river and avenge the raid after sixteen years. He asked me, "Would you go with me, Bobby? Glenn was your friend."

"Yes, Mr. Nevill, I will," was my answer because I felt badly and I surely was sorry for him. After Glenn's death, he had always treated me as a son. But I didn't go back until 1963.

☆ ☆ ☆

At 11:20 p.m. on March 26, Captain Anderson answered his phone in Marfa. He said later that he had a premonition about the message before he answered. The call, which had been relayed from Valentine by way of Lobo from Sergeant Simpson at Green River (also called the Upper Nevill Ranch), said that Ramón Castillo had raced in on a lathered horse, bareback, to tell them bandits were raiding the Lower Nevill place.

Our first sergeant ran into the barracks and yelled, "Nevill's ranch has been raided. The captain wants all of you there, quick."

We had, in the back of our minds at least, been expecting and fearing just such a message and now that it had arrived we went into violent action. As we dressed, we talked, the consensus being that the raid was made to avenge the Porvenir murders. When we were dressed, it was a race to the stables.

Emergency moves were always made Full Pack, by which I mean, in addition to rifles and pistols and canteens, we each took two blankets, two bandoleers of rifle ammunition, and emergency field rations. By the shortest distance, it was seventeen miles to the ranch on a bad road, but we knew the shortcuts—and there was a moon that night. The men with the slowest horses got to the ranch by 1:30 in the morning, so you may be sure it was a wild ride over those rough trails. However, the night was very cold, and the horses were fresh, and seemed to enjoy it. Not knowing what we were riding into, our feelings for the Nevills urged us on and inspired every man to want to do his damnedest.

At the wire gate in the horse trap, we pulled up and dismounted. This was a quarter mile from the house. We listened intently, but all we could hear at first were the doves. However, in a few moments, we thought we could hear groans, and then loud yelling, and we could make out the words, "Don't shoot."

No one could recognize the voice, but we opened the gate and started toward the house, leading our horses. The yelling came again, and now we could make out, "Don't shoot, boys, I'm coming up," and it sounded like Mr. Nevill's voice.

Someone yelled back, "Come on up." Every noise on that cold night seemed to bounce up and down the river bottom. We could hear the groans distinctly by then, and we knew they were coming from the house.

Leaving our horses in the charge of a detail, we walked on. When we were within fifty feet of the house, we heard the yell come out of the bosque again, saying, "Don't shoot," and then Mr. Nevill came running out of the brush.

We could see his face was covered with blood. His first words as he reached us were, "I'm afraid they killed that boy. I've got to find that boy." Seldom had any of us ever seen Mr. Nevill without a hat and he would have been hard to recognize except for his voice. His hair was matted with sweat and blood, and full of leaves.

Now the groans came louder than ever, and the captain, who had a flashlight in his hand, threw the beam toward the sounds, but all we could see was a large pile of cottonseed cake.[47] Behind the cake, we found Glenn sprawled on his back. It only took a glance to tell that he was in bad shape. His right leg was doubled under his body, and he was completely covered with blood.

We tried to hold Mr. Nevill back, but he wouldn't be held. As he knelt beside his boy, we were deeply touched. This was the first terrible price to be paid for the awful orgy carried out at Porvenir just thirty-three days earlier. Poor Glenn was beyond pain and hearing then, but anyone can imagine the anguish of his father as he sobbed over and over, "Oh, God, son, what will I tell your mother and sister?"

As we thought of what had caused this terrible thing, you can bet our blood boiled. Glenn had been shot in the right leg between the hip and knee, causing a compound fracture, and had fallen in such a manner that his foot was under his back. For a moment we hoped the leg was his only trouble. Someone got a mattress from the porch, and we pulled Mr. Nevill to his feet. But when we started to lift Glenn onto the mattress, we discovered the entire back of his head had been shot away, and a piece of scalp as large as your hand hung only by some skin.

We did succeed in keeping Mr. Nevill from seeing this as we got Glenn onto the mattress, carried him into the house, placed him on the bed, and lit a lamp.

One moment Mr. Nevill would cry, and the next he would curse the bandits and then the Rangers with wild fury, and then he would drop to his knees beside the bed and sob, "It'll be all right, son, it'll be all right."

Poor Mr. Nevill was sitting by the bed near Glenn, with his head in his gnarled, bloody hands. We built a big fire in the fireplace, but the room was cold. The captain sat over by the fire with his head down, deeply affected. It was a very sad time, and every man in the room knew exactly why this terrible vengeance had been wreaked upon this family.

Soon the outside guard and the search detail, which had been busy ever since our arrival, reported that no one was in the area, and that tracks at the ford indicated a great many horses and cattle had crossed into Mexico. It was about eight hours since Glenn had been shot, and we were all sure even expert medical services could not have saved his life. Still, all of the time since our arrival he had continued to moan loudly and his pulse was strong. We were thankful his eyes were closed, as it was hard enough for us to hear him moaning, "Mama."

The excitement up until this time over Glenn and Mr. Nevill had led us to overlook the Castillos, but then, with a great deal of apprehension, we crossed to their end of the house. The inside door was open, and as we opened the screen door and threw the flashlight beam inside, a terrible scream rang out—a child's scream—and we saw huddled against the wall across from the fireplace the little boy, who was screaming wildly. No doubt he had been in there, terrified, for hours.

We slowly gathered around him, calling his name, Joe—his real name was José, but we called him Joe. Although he was hysterical, he realized who we were, and one of the boys picked him up in his arms. It was at that point we discovered the most terrible part of the Nevill raid.

There was a table in the center of the room, running north and south, but it was only three feet from the west wall, and behind the table, in a sitting position on the floor, sat the body of Rosa Castillo. Her head, turned slightly to the side, rested against a log of the wall. Her legs were extended straight out, and her hands were resting on the rough floor. She had been shot through the head and heart—either shot would have been fatal. Her clothing had been disarranged, and a stick of wood had been forced into her body.

She was almost naked and had been dead a long time. Lying on each side of her, on the floor, were her breasts, which had been neatly cut from her body, looking like bloody, inverted funnels. She was covered with blood and dirt, and by the bruises, we could see she had been beaten before her death. It was an ugly, terrifying site, the most horrible mutilation any of us had ever seen, and we wondered what the little boy had witnessed.

We took José into the other part of the house where a fire had been built. He had a bloody welt on his scalp that led us to hope that the little fellow might have been unconscious when his mother was killed. Later he told his Daddy that a man had hit him with a gun. There is no reason to doubt that they intended to kill him too, and had thought he was really dead.

All of the people dead and badly hurt there had been our good friends. Many times, in bad weather, we had spent the night with them and, of course, caused them extra work, especially Rosa, but they were always glad to have us and we were happy to be there. We appreciated their kindness and friendship. Now they were dead or dying, and knowing who had caused the raid made it even more painful. It is beyond my power of comprehension how anyone could have seen such a sight without being bitter.

There was no moon then, and it was pitch black. Everybody's nerves were on edge, but all we could do was try and comfort Mr. Nevill and that little boy and wait for daylight. We had found no trace of Ramón, and since the patrol had failed to tell us how they had learned of the raid, the captain sent a patrol of six men to the Upper Ranch to find out if the patrol was all right and to call Van Horn and notify Nevill's friends. Captain Anderson also instructed the patrol that Mr. Nevill wanted the family doctor notified. He requested that cars or an ambulance come down to the Upper Ranch.

Glenn died quietly at 6:00 o'clock in the morning, while it was still dark outside. We knew he was dead because the murmuring stopped. I don't believe any of us have gone through a sadder hour since. At daylight, the patrol going to the Upper Nevill Place met a delegation from Van Horn that included many of Nevill's friends and his doctor. They were within six miles of the ranch. They had made it down that rough trail in a white truck and a 1917 Oldsmobile, bringing Ramón Castillo and the patrol from the Upper Nevill Ranch.

After Glenn died, Mr. Nevill became quiet and I, for one, imagined he was silently praying. In a short time he looked up and sort of shuddered before he began telling us what had happened. Until that time none of us had mentioned the bandits.

"When Charley whinnied," he began, "and I looked up and saw them in the river, I was so frozen with fear I couldn't even think right. Behind me there were three loaded rifles, but I never thought of them, and when they crossed the ford and began jumping off their horses I know that I yelled, 'Come on,' and ran out of the east side of the porch.

"I didn't even think of Rosa or that little boy. I just don't know what in the hell happened to me. I went plumb crazy, I guess. It seemed like Glenn was right behind me, but I didn't see him. I've heard of fellows going crazy in a tight spot, but I never thought it would happen to me.

"When I cleared the corner of the house," he continued, "I heard Glenn cry out and I glanced around and saw him fall by that pile of cake. God, it was awful. Just then I saw them damn Mexicans jump out the porch door, and when they saw me, they started to shoot and yell like demons. That very second was the first time I had thought of the rifles, but it was too late, so I ran for the bosque as fast as I could. Thousands of times I have thought out every move I'd make in a fix like that, and I figured I could always kill at least ten Mexicans before they got me. There's no use in trying to tell you boys about it—I don't know. I just don't know."[48]

With that, he buried his head beside Glenn and sobbed for a while. Pretty soon he started in again, "I know that I am not a coward, and right now I'd gladly give my life if I could bring back that boy. I wish that they had killed me, too. I just don't know how to face his mother. Just last night she told me, 'Be sure and take good care of our boy,' when I left her. I'm not afraid of Mexicans, you all know that, I've run into lots of them in that damn bosque and never before did the bastards scare me. I just stood there like a dummy and counted them instead of shooting at them. I knew the Mendozas and Rodriquez right off."

He said the Mendozas knew just where everything was kept and he said that he had heard them yelling to the men who were in the bosque searching for him to be sure they found him and killed him because he was "*Muy Mal*," very bad.

"I wasn't scared, but I guess I was crazy. Before I reached the bosque, it was nearly dark, and although several shots came pretty close, I wasn't hit at all. I fell once, jumped up and ran until the brush hid me. You all know how that damn catclaw and mesquite can tear you, and I didn't dodge any of it.

"I could hear the yelling and shooting up at the house, but it was so dark the house was only a blur. Still, I could see the gun flashes. I found a cottonwood log partly buried by brush and leaves, and threw myself down beside it and pulled the brush over me. I was wet with sweat. I lay there a moment, and seemed to be getting my senses back. I tried to decide what to do.

"Then I heard a terrible scream up there at the house, and I knew it must be Rosa. I was sick over what they were doing to her and that poor little boy. I reached in my pocket and found my knife and opened it, and about that time I heard brush popping and a Mexican say, 'Right in there.' Then I had my senses back and my nerve, too, and I crouched so I could jump up quickly.

"I hoped that they would come close enough so I could grab one. I intended to cut his throat, grab his rifle, and I felt as though I could kill them all. They came close, all right, but not close enough, and I could see that there were two of them.

"Their footsteps finally died away, and then in a few moments, I could hear horses moving around, and the rattle of equipment and the squeak of leather, so I figured they were getting ready to leave. I heard quite a commotion in the back of the horse trap, and the bawling of cattle, which meant they were taking my heifers. They must have taken them all, for pretty soon I heard splashing and cattle bawling at the river, and I knew they were headed for Mexico.

"Did you find Rosa?" he asked, but before anyone answered he went on, "I sure hope they didn't kill her. That would be awful, but I know they done something terrible to her on account of the way she screamed. You know she wasn't the screaming kind."

I was right beside him, and he looked up at me with a question in his eyes, but he quickly said, "If something has happened to her, don't tell me. I just couldn't stand any more.

"They weren't here an hour, I know, but it seemed like a lifetime to me. After the noise at the ford stopped, I started up to the house. Before I had taken two steps, I heard you boys, and I know now that I had been in the bosque for a long time. I guess I must have passed out, because I was lying on the ground when I heard you, and I don't rightly know how I got there. I was so stiff and cold, I couldn't hardly yell at first."

Just then we heard a commotion outside. We ran out to find Ramón on Glenn's horse, Shorty, bareback, talking to the guard. He was asking about Rosa and his boy, but they didn't tell him anything except that the little boy would be all right, and we took him inside. He took José in his arms and went and sat in the corner. He must have known that Rosa was dead because he didn't ask again.

After a while, Mr. Nevill asked, "Ramón, how did you get away?"

For a moment Ramón didn't answer, then he said, "When they came, I thought you and Glenn could hold them off, and I ran around the north end of the house into the horse trap. I thought I'd get one of the horses and go for the patrol. Well, I finally did, but I had a hard time catching a horse. They were in the back corner. I think the shooting had them spooked.

"I nearly caught one twice, but each time he broke away and ran off, then the third time, I got them in the corner and talked to them, and then I got my hand on Shorty's rump and he turned to run, but I got hold of his mane, and then his nose, and held on. He was sure scared, but I talked to him and in a little while the other three came back.

"Then he stood quietly while I tore up my shirt. I used that and my belt to make a hackamore. I led him over to that arroyo where the fence was tied down, and loosened the rock that holds it down, and by holding up on the wires, I got Shorty to go under it.

"While I was getting him under that fence, I heard a scream and I knew it must be Rosa." Ramón stopped then, and he didn't say another word for what seemed to be an eternity, but he finally continued.

"I led Shorty up to a rock and got on, but he threw me off right away. I hung onto the reins, though, and petted him and talked to him, and while I did this I heard them Mexicans close by in the trap. I think they took all of the other horses and the heifers too.

"I got on Shorty again and held him up as tight as I could and petted him some more, and then I let him go; and he didn't pitch, but I walked him 'til I got him to the trail and then put him into a running walk for a little way, and pretty soon a lope and from there to a run, and I ran him all the way to the Upper Place.

"I stopped a half mile out and yelled until the patrol told me to come in and then I told them about the bandits and asked them to come back with me, but they had to use the telephone and wouldn't give me a rifle, or come down with me, either.

"After a couple of hours they decided to go down with me about 5:00 p.m. if nobody came from Van Horn, but before that, the two cars and the people came, so we all came down together. When we met the other patrol, they told us that the bandits were all gone, so I ran Shorty all the way down here."

So Ramón had been the first link in the communications to us. What he had told of his escape and ride for help, he told with many hesitations and sometimes in a voice that was barely audible, but realizing what he must know, it was remarkable that he was able to talk at all.

Within the half hour two patrols and a truck came in. It was sunup. The doctor was a man past sixty who had been the Nevill family doctor when Glenn was born. Although he was badly shaken, he treated Mr. Nevill for shock and the little boy too, dressed his wound, and then gave them both a sedative.

We decided to fix Glenn and Rosa up as well as we possibly could for the long ride back to Van Horn in the truck. The hospital corpsman helped the doctor, and we saw to it that Mr. Nevill and Ramón were out of the way while they worked. Rosa was placed in the truck first, and secured, and then Glenn.

Mr. Nevill broke down for a moment, but Ramón looked at the ground and said nothing; neither did he show any outward emotion, yet we all knew that he had worshipped Rosa. Some people are made that way, but many of us could hardly hold back the tears. When everything was ready, they pulled out, and Mr. Nevill, Ramón, and the little boy went along on that sad journey to Van Horn.

We had loaded all the personal belongings of both families into the truck, and now the ranch house that had always been a welcome sight to us was as deserted and ghostlike as Pilares and Porvenir. There was nothing left on the river anymore except Mr. Nevill's cattle. Two months before, there had been five friendly human habitations in our lonely fifty-mile stretch. Now everyone had either been killed or forced to leave.

On the river, Mr. Nevill's presence had given us a feeling of security and until that night, we thought he and Glenn would have fought to the death. It must be that a raid by armed, mounted men in the night, shooting and yelling like banshees, strikes such terror into the very souls of those who experience it, that even though they had been men of courage, they could emerge branded as cowards.

Chapter 10—Pursuit

The patrol from the upper adobe brought verbal instructions from Colonel Langhorne. Ten pack mules and supplies were being sent by special train from Marfa to Lobo, accompanied by ten men from B Troop, two packers, and three scouts who had worked all over Chihuahua, and were familiar with the country to the south. They would arrive overland by noon, and when they did, we were to take up the trail of the bandits in Chihuahua and annihilate them.

It was the morning of March 27. While we waited for the pack outfit, we scouted both sides of the river, and discovered where the men had waited in the bosque before the raid. Judging by the evidence, they must have been there more than a couple of hours. When they crossed into Mexico, they had headed straight south toward a saddle in the little Sierra Madre where the old trail crossed toward the old T.O. Ranch.

The outfit rode in just about noon, telling us they had missed the Rim Rock Trail and had really pushed the mules—and indeed, the animals showed by their sweat that something had really pushed them. There were four pack mules loaded with provisions and five thousand rounds of Springfield ammunition, ten cavalrymen from B Troop and a lieutenant, and two .30 caliber machine guns which were carried on a horse, tripods and all. They were assigned to B Troop and were the property of the machine gun group. We were happy to see the scouts that were sent—Drake, Beall, and Bell—all good men to have along.

After watering all the stock at the river and filling our canteens, we hit their trail. That first day, I, along with Drake, Bell, and ten picked men, rode the advanced guard. We were thankful to be in the lead for many reasons but in particular, because of the dust. There were eighty-five cavalrymen, ten pack mules, four packers, and three scouts, 102 animals in all, and toward the end of the column the dust was bad. The trail was the usual single-file Indian trail, and it was rough country, as most of Chihuahua is. The column was about a half-mile in length, with the pack train bringing up the rear. The only living things we ran across within fifteen miles of the river that first day were bobcats, quail, wild burros, and horses.

The raiders had a start of at least sixteen hours, but they were driving cattle and horses—how many we could not be sure. Mr. Nevill had three horses, ten heifers, and a milk cow in the trap, and we had made sure they were all gone before we left. Since the range cattle were never bedded on the river, we were quite certain none had been found, even if the raiders had looked for them.

Right now, I will say that Mr. Nevill had always run over two thousand head, with only the water gaps of the Rio Grande separating Texas and Mexico. The stretch of river his cattle ran and watered on was as wild and desolate as any in America, and as I have said before, hardly a day passed, particularly in the summertime, that fifty or more armed men of some kind or other didn't pass up or down that river within sight of those cattle. Some were Villistas, some Carranzistas, some bandits, and sometimes they were just families on the move. Any of them could have crossed the river in ten loping strides of a horse, and run off with five or six head of cattle, if that had been in their minds. Yet in five years, Nevill had never lost a single head of stock to bandits.

The raiders had taken rifles, ammunition, three pairs of chaps, spurs, two new catch ropes, and every item of clothing as well as all of the food, and the place was always well stocked. Their trail led south through the foothills in the direction of a low gap in the little Sierra Madre. We knew we were twelve hours behind them but we were able to make good time, in spite of the fact that the patrol was moving single file.

At about 3:00 p.m. we found their first camp. They had picked a beautiful spot. There were several large trees and boulders and on the canyon's edge, a spring. They had made twenty miles or more that first night before making camp in the foothills of the little Sierra Madre, just below the saddle we were headed for. By the sign left, mostly horse droppings, we determined they had been in camp at least twelve hours. We already knew the bandits had taken some of the Nevill livestock. Two old, beat-up Chihuahua saddles were found in the brush where they had been discarded. The bandits were now riding on the three saddles stolen from the Nevills. According to the scouts, they were only driving about ten head of cattle, so all they had taken were the heifers.

One of the Nevill heifers had been butchered on the ground in a crude Indian manner. Only a part of the meat had been taken, and the evidence showed wild animals and buzzards had really enjoyed a feast. In fact, heavily loaded buzzards sat all over the canyon. As always I found them repulsive, but I suppose they are necessary, and I have never doubted God's wisdom in placing them here.

There was very little left of the carcass. Most of the hide had perhaps been used green to wrap stirrups and saddle horns, and the little that was left had been dragged all around by animals. On a piece of hide we found Mr. Nevill's brand which he called stacked V. We found an old pair of shoes, some clothing, several pairs of socks, and a pint whiskey bottle. Mr. Nevill had bought a bottle of whiskey in Van Horn and brought it home with him. No one drank it that I knew of, but he had looked for whiskey the night before Glenn died.

We lost few minutes in the camp. The saddle of the mountain appeared to be about a mile ahead. Just after leaving the bandit camp, we came to a most unusual phenomenon. In a dense grove of cedar and jack pine, there were five huge flat rocks fifty feet in diameter standing up out of the ground about table height. It was surprising to see they were also almost level on top.

Captain Anderson called a halt to examine the strange formation, so we took the opportunity to wipe the dust from our horses' nostrils with a damp rag. This little kindness is next to a drink of cool water for your horse.

The air that high up was cool and invigorating. We ate lunch in the saddle, and were anxious to reach a place where fires could be built so we might at least have hot coffee. But Drake told us that it should be another twelve miles before we would find water. In the valley, scattered over its length, there had been five ranch towns, one of which should be dead ahead of us to the south. It was called Domingo.

When we reached the mountaintop, the scene was breathtaking. The slope of the mountain extended to the south about two miles, and ended at the edge of a wide, flat valley. Beyond the valley to the south rose the jagged peaks of the Sierra Madre (mother mountains) which are a rare sight, no matter where you see them from. We were about seven thousand feet above the valley floor. The distance across the valley from our height appeared to be ten or twelve miles, but Drake, who knew this part of Chihuahua well, told us it was near to sixty miles and always a good day's ride.

This broad, beautiful valley, so the scouts informed us, had been the main T.O. Ranch holdings. We were high in the foothills and everything as far as the eye could see was green with cedar and juniper. Manzanita grew profusely and the bright red berries blended beautifully with the green. Even that high up, there were dove and quail, as well as bobcats, and we had ridden right into three large herds of deer. It was wild and primitive, and perfect for an ambusher to hide in. They said that it was fifty miles wide and 150 miles in length. Never have I seen a more beautiful valley, although there are surely such beautiful places in both Montana and Wyoming. Perhaps it was the wild loneliness of the vast uninhabited country.

★ ★ ★

As we looked with the glasses, we saw what seemed to be a monstrous wheat field, and even in March, the old grass was waving stirrup high, with not a living thing to eat it except roving bands of wild horses, burros, and Spanish mules. In a moment we located buildings far out on the valley floor. Everyone thought it was a large ranch, but the scouts informed us that it was Domingo, which had been a deserted ghost town since 1912. Drake said that he had headquartered there when he worked for the T.O. Ranch.

The outfit with the pack mules had already made roughly sixty miles since daylight, but the mules were good ones, and not heavily loaded. Every one of us was dead tired, having had no sleep the previous night, so we decided to go to old Domingo and camp. The town was not yet visible to the naked eye, and even with the glasses it seemed to blend with the countryside. There was no dust anywhere, or any other sign of mounted men, so we moved out of the foothills and drew closer to the old town.

When we arrived after sundown, we found two windmills, one of which was pumping a trickle of water and groaning something awful from long neglect and lack of oil. The water from the windmill tasted all right, but it took a long time to fill a canteen. There was a dirt tank that the trickle of water ran into, and we debated about letting the horses drink from it. A few of us wet our hands and touched our tongues to the water, and it tasted awful.

One of the men took a stick and was poking into the tank to see how deep it was, when he came up with what looked like a dead animal—at least it was hide with hair on it—and that sort of made us water tasters blink a little. Someone said, "Hell, that water's poison," and everybody agreed with him. The horses needed water, but the weather was really cool, so they didn't get any.

We made a quick run through the nine old buildings to make sure no one was there. It was dark now. We made strong coffee, but we ate bully beef cold with a little hardtack, and then put the fire out. Each of us had a blanket, and this night we used our saddle blankets, too. We were used to sleeping on the ground, but that night the temperature went almost below freezing, I'm sure, and there was no bed of coals or fire to sleep beside.

The entire place had a smoky, decayed smell about it, and even the coffee didn't taste right, but it was hot and strong. There was no way to corral the animals, so we hobbled the mules and put them on a picket line by the packers. We agreed that every man would sleep with his horse, which resulted in a long, half-awake night. Each man could stake his horse near his blankets, or he could hold him with a neck rope. It all depended on how well you knew your horse and yourself. I have slept well many nights holding my horse.

While in regular cavalry barracks, such as Fort Bliss, the Eighth regiment under Colonel Langhorne used white halter shanks strictly for dress and parade purposes. This was a pure white rope with one end attached to the halter ring if a halter was used. Otherwise, it was snapped into the ring of the snaffle bit. The other end was placed around the neck of the horse near the withers and the end wrapped around the other side of the rope in a regular hangman's knot. It served as a sort of martingale.

It certainly dressed up any horse and it surely made other regiments envious. The Seventh Cavalry called us the White Halter Shank Outfit, but they were jealous.

On a trip like the one we were on, and even on patrol, we carried the halter shank, which was five-eighths inches in thickness and ten feet long. It was of the very finest manila quality and made an excellent neck rope to tie a horse by at any time. It was soft, and extremely strong. I would place the rope around my horse's neck, close-up toward his ears and tie it there with a slip-proof half-bowline knot. In the other end I would tie a loop also, using a half-bowline just large enough to slip over my hand. Then I would hold the rope in my hand with the loop around my wrist. You soon learn to quiet your horse if he becomes frightened or restless, without even fully waking up. Yes, the halter shank was good for a great many purposes besides beautifying your horse in a parade.

That night, we were thirty-five miles deep in Villa-Carranza territory, and with a group of heavily armed bandits perhaps less than eight miles away, we weren't likely to sleep much anyway. Our only authority or protection was the flimsy Hot Pursuit Treaty,[49] and we all knew that only a Carranza officer of high rank would recognize our right to be there. Anyone else would consider us invaders, so it was to our interest not to be caught, especially by federal troops and cause an international incident.

None of us wanted any fire to be spotted, and since we were deep in Villa-Carranza territory—to say nothing of the bandits—it was a spooky night. A little wind came up, and the windmill ran like mad, and since we were camped close to it, I believe every man in the outfit got his canteen full of water. The old windmill cried and groaned, and there were more strange noises that night than any of us had ever heard before.

Some kind of animal must have come up pretty close, because whatever it was—it couldn't have been any horse, dog, or burro—spooked the horses and they stood the rest of the night pointing their ears in its direction. Part of the awful noise during the night was made by some pieces of galvanized iron that had blown off the roof of one of the old houses, and were lying way out on the flat, as well as other pieces that were coming loose which the wind kept whipping up and down.

When we were saddled and ready to move on at daylight, we thawed out at the fire the cook had built for coffee. It was then March 28. Some of us rode around the old place a few moments. Seven of the buildings were made of vertical boards and two were of adobe. All of them had galvanized iron roofing, and about half of the boards were gone from the houses. One was in pretty good shape, and had been lived in quite elaborately and very recently, too, but there was nobody home now for sure, and there probably never would be again. Still, the smell of human habitation was so strong that we expected someone to say, "Good morning," although our only greeting came from a pack rat that scampered across the dirt floor.

There had been large, stout pole corrals, but squatters and campers had used up most of the corrals for firewood. Out a short distance from the buildings, there were five graves, one of which couldn't have been more than a month old. It had a crudely made wooden cross stuck in the ground. On many of the large corral posts was the T.O. brand and in one of the corrals there was a snubbing post ten inches in diameter which was branded all over with the letters T.O.

We had left the bandits' trail at the foothills the evening before, and now we headed back to pick it up again. It was so cold, we beat our arms around our bodies to prevent our hands from becoming numb. The scouts had their work cut out for them because we had to be certain the trail wasn't a decoy or a trap. We followed the trail up the canyon a half-mile or more before we came to a *rincon*, or sunken place in the floor of the canyon. It was like a slightly sunken garden about one hundred feet in diameter. There was a stream of water in the canyon further up. We could see the water without glasses but there by the *rincon,* the canyon was dry and the water had gone underground.

It was an hour after sunup, and fifteen miles from where we had camped, when we found their second camp. We found more old clothing, and several peach cans, also an empty flour sack. We envied them the breakfast they must have had: beefsteak, peaches, Dutch oven bread or tortillas and, of course, coffee with sugar. The ashes of their fires were still warm, but we knew they were at least four hours ahead of us, and had the advantage of knowing where they were headed. The bandits had turned southeast and followed the edge of the hills.

In that small area, it took about an hour to water our horses, since only two could drink at a time. Before we left, we dumped our water and filled all our canteens.

Just below the camp they had turned back toward the mountains, and we were quite certain they were headed toward the Pilares presidio to make a stand. It was only a guess, but there would be no other reason to cross those mountains again. We knew they must have seen us the evening before, and they simply intended to go where we couldn't follow—either that, or lead us into an ambush higher up. Up in the foothills we could see for a long way, and we thoroughly searched the side of the mountain, but couldn't pick up a thing except what appeared to be about twenty deer off to the right. When the scouts who had ridden up the canyon came back, they reported the trail turned up out of the canyon a half-mile further. They also stated it would be quite a scramble getting out of the canyon at that point since there was no trail and the canyon was very steep.

The scouts thought it would be easier to climb out from where we were, and the captain agreed. When we were ready and the advance guard had moved ahead five or six hundred yards with the scouts, we climbed up out of the canyon and took up the trail again. The ridge we were on gave very poor footing—there was nothing but a rocky shale along the lip—and that was where the bandits had begun their ascent. Perhaps they had picked the hardest trail of all, believing we might not be able to follow.

It was hell on the horses, as we were going over some bad places. They were following the lip of the canyon which all seemed to be shale rock, and one slip could send you to the bottom. This was real bad country, but we didn't underestimate our horses. The horse I was riding was one of the very best—gentle, fast, and sure-footed. The scouts up ahead were both riding short, stout steel dusts, good mountain horses that did as much wailing going up that ridge as we did.

It took us four hours to make six miles, but we were nearing the top, riding through scrub cedar and lots of jack pines, as well as larger pine trees. The nearer we got to the head of the canyon, the rougher the country became. It was less than a mile to the top, when ahead of us we saw a cluster of large boulders as big as houses. There were also a few big pine trees nearby, and we thought if the bandits planned an ambush, that would be the place, but we were heading into the wind, and our horses told us there were no bandits up there.

The bandits had evidently circled the ledge of rock that we found ourselves up against, which had the scouts stopped for a moment. Above us, though, we could see the trail plainly in the shale rock, so Drake looped a rope around his horse's neck, and then climbed up on a ledge on foot. He clucked to his horse and gave a little pull on the rope, and up he went, clawing for a foothold and throwing rocks in every direction, but he made it, and cleared such a trail that the tail end of our column rode up on their horses.

The mountainside became wildly beautiful again, and the higher we climbed, the more exciting it was. At the top, we dismounted on the little bench and looked for a while with our glasses. It really was wild, beautiful country. Buzzards had been circling over the deep canyon, and a few of us walked over to look down into that dangerous hole, which we could see ended in a box a little way ahead. Down in the canyon we could see water and a lot of green vegetation. It was all of three hundred feet straight down.

About two hundred feet down the canyon from where we stood, we spotted a cow lying between two rocks, belly up with her head under her, and then we saw a horse with a saddle, lying on its side, and about twenty feet from the horse, a man lying face down. The fall had crushed all of them, and with the glasses we could see blood around each dead body. There was no movement, of course, but we dropped a few rocks, and when nothing moved, we were sure they were all dead. We couldn't get to them, so we marked off one bandit and another Nevill heifer.

We pushed on and soon topped out on the little Sierra Madre again, and just as we reached the summit, we jumped an enormous herd of deer. There must have been two hundred. The view from the top was the most fantastic I have ever seen. The air was so clear that with the naked eye, we could see for fifty miles. The wild panorama took in all of that slope of the mountain in Chihuahua and all of the Rim Rock country of Texas, while to the south we could see the giant wheat field and the Sierra Madre.

There had been extensive timber cutting, and all of the stumps told us it had been a long time ago. There was quite a clearing, but although the bandit outfit was definitely on that slope, we couldn't pick up a single moving thing with our glasses. There wasn't the slightest doubt of their presence somewhere between the river and where we stood, but I will give the seasoned Mexican credit for having an uncanny ability to travel across country leaving little trail, raising a minimum amount of dust, and staying hidden ninety percent of the time. In that respect they are almost equal to the Apaches.

Think back to the 1916 Punitive Expedition led by General Pershing, which was in Chihuahua to kill Pancho Villa. Pershing had the best of scouts, several airplanes, and ten thousand well-mounted men. But after one full year, they had failed to get within twenty miles of Villa or his followers. By constantly out-maneuvering our cavalry and scouts, the Mexicans proved to be among the world's best.

As soon as we started moving, we found an old wagon road that must have been used at some time to haul logs and wood to Porvenir and Pilares. In five minutes, we reached a position where we could see the long dark stretch of the river bosque, then Pilares and the presidio. The distance, we guessed, was about sixteen miles.

Pilares had been quite a town just seven years before. A federal garrison had been maintained at the presidio, which we knew was still in good condition. It was a circular wall of adobe brick about thirty inches wide and five and a half feet high. It was about a hundred feet in diameter, with two portals or entrances.

Situated on the rise of ground at the back, or south of the town, the walls had portholes, and would protect horses and men from any direction. We knew it was abandoned, but as we drew closer, we had the feeling that the bandits would make their stand right there behind those walls, if they made one at all.

When the column was about two miles from Pilares, we saw a black smoke signal go up from the presidio, but could hear no noise or explosion. We wondered what its purpose had been. The horses were taking on new life, for they could smell the water. We needed water, and the horses needed water, and now the river was in sight. When the scouts and seven other men riding as flankers and advance guards reached the river trail, they waited for us to close up. No one had seen any sign of life at all, and I believe that we had all strained our eyes. From the droppings on the trail, we could tell they couldn't be more than an hour ahead of us, and they were still driving Nevill's cattle and horses.

We started bunching up at the edge of the bosque, preparing to make the run through the narrow passage between the ridge and the river so we could reach the village of Pilares, Chihuahua, and the presidio in back of it. The ridge ran to within twenty feet of the water, about seventy-five feet high. We were bunched up in a wide, flat canyon, and decided to pass the end of the bluff as fast as possible, and then charge the town and presidio.

It was about five hundred yards to the presidio, and we were sure the raiders were holed up there. The riverbank was high at that point, and even though the flow was normal, it must have been eight feet down to the water. But we had no intention of giving the horses water then, because if we did, we would have to run them. Furthermore, we didn't want to be caught out in the river and become targets.

I took my rifle out of the scabbard and checked it. I had one shell in the chamber and five in the magazine, but I made sure the extra clips were free in my belt. About ten of us made the start, with the other groups close behind. No one seemed to care what we ran into.

Well, we simply flew toward the end of that bluff, knowing our horses were good for top speed all the way to the presidio, about a quarter of a mile away. Then, just as we were about to pass the end of the bluff, all hell broke loose. The bandits were hidden in trenches on top of the bluff, and it sounded as though fifty rifles had been fired at the same instant. It was the first hot, concentrated hail of lead that any of us had ever experienced. The sound that first reached us was very similar to wide boards being dropped flat onto other boards.

It was a rough ten seconds, I'll tell you. Bullets were singing and whining everywhere, and all we could see were puffs of smoke, so we broke and ran to get out of their range. As I have said before, my horse was fast, and he was in a dead run, I can assure you. All at once, both of us hit the ground hard. It seemed the horse stood on his head for a minute—but I guess it wasn't even a second—and I thought for sure he was going to fall on me in spite of all I could do, but he barely touched my foot.

The bridle reins were still in my hands as we got to our feet about the same time. He was snorting and trembling so badly that I couldn't get close to him. He kept backing away like I was a plumb stranger. The reins seemed awfully long, when I saw they had been broken. I never used a curb bit on him, just a straight bar, and I had the habit of tying the reins together—quite a few of us did—in order to have the reins right where we wanted them on the neck, and leave both hands free for holding a rifle when shooting from horseback.

I kept talking to him, but he looked wild-eyed and still trembled. When I did get up to him, I kept him between me and the bluff, but I petted him, stroking his neck and wondering what had thrown him, and why the bridle reins had broken. I discovered blood on my hands, and although I couldn't feel anything, I supposed that I must have been shot. By that time, the shots had stopped, and we had been a standing target for a long time.

I tied the reins together quickly, and as I was making the tie, I discovered the horse had been shot in the neck just below where the mane starts, about six inches in front of the withers. It had been an almost perfect job of creasing, but that Mexican, of course, had been trying to give us more than a crease. The bullet, which had not gone through his neck, had been what cut my bridle reins.

I glanced at my outfit. The ambush had caused a lot of confusion. Even to me, as I read this over, it seems as though several moments had elapsed, but it all had taken less than a minute. Two of the pack mules were hobbling on three legs, and later, one of them had to be shot. The bullet had hit him in the hip and leg, breaking the pastern joint just below the fetlock. We later estimated over a hundred shots had been fired at us, and up until that moment there hadn't been a man or horse down besides Brownie and me.

After the initial shock, we were aware that every man had been firing with a little madness. Again we started a wild charge, for we could hear horses snorting and running up on the ridge. Around me at that second were about twelve of my friends, one of whom was Ted Alberts. We had hardly gotten started again, when Alberts let out a grunt that sounded like, "Ugh-ugh," and then we heard the crack of a rifle, and saw a puff of smoke about halfway up the side of the bluff. Poor Alberts slid off his horse onto his head, and we knew he had been hit hard.

We jumped off our horses, and a few men poured a deadly fire toward the spot where we saw the smoke puffs, while the rest of us examined Alberts. He had been killed instantly. The bullet had gone into his left breast and left a large, gaping hole under the shoulder blade. Someone made the remark, "That son-of-a-bitch has one of Nevill's rifles," but he was wrong, as we soon discovered. None of the Savage rifles the raiders had taken were ever recovered.

We were not panicky then; we were plain mad. The rest of the outfit closed up, and all who had glasses tried to locate the sniper, who had been less than two hundred yards away. We couldn't see him, but we could see a trench and stone breastwork where we knew he was hidden. Later that day, we found out there were trenches on both sides of the ridge, and two long ones on top where most of the bandits had hidden when the ambush started. All of these trenches were part of the defenses of the presidio.

The men kept firing at the trench, and just as we decided to go up from all directions, one man jumped out and started to the top. He didn't get ten feet until he, too, died instantly, having been hit in at least nine vital spots, we found out when we finally reached his body.

Our burning problem now was the running horses we could hear, so we left a detail to place Alberts on his horse and cross the river with him, while seventy-five mounted men took off for a slope that could take us to the top of that ridge.

To the reader it may seem like a lot of time had been wasted, but I can assure you everything I have described so far had taken less than two minutes. No one lets any grass grow under his feet at a time like that.

The bandits must have had their horses hidden under a lip of the bluff, and after firing and emptying their rifles twice, they were able to get to their horses out of our sight. When we reached the top of the bluff, they had about a six hundred yard start on us. The ridge was flat and fairly smooth, so we spread out and fired on the run from horseback, knocking down five of them, and finishing them off as we closed up to overtake them.

As nearly as we ever made out, there were fourteen mounted bandits to start with, racing toward the mountains. We were not able to close the gap, so our captain (who was right up there with us) yelled, "Hit the ground!" and from a prone position we knocked down four more of them, leaving the others out of range. If our horses hadn't been so winded, we could have gotten them all, but they were almost done for, as they had gone without water for over thirty hours.

From the ones that escaped, it was easy to pick out Nevill's three dun-colored horses, and also a snow-white horse, the like of which we couldn't remember ever having seen on the river before. Mr. Nevill had told us about it. White horses were not a bit popular down there.

It may seem strange, but of all the bandits killed that day, only two had .30-.30 rifles—and short saddle guns at that. All of the rest had old Mauser short-barreled saddle guns. None of their saddles were any good, but I suppose all of us took some kind of trinket, and of course we kept all of the rifles.

Counting the Mexicans who had fallen into the canyon, eleven were dead. Later, in the trench they had been shooting from, we discovered another man who had been shot accidentally, we assumed, by the men who had been covering us. He had been shot in the forehead, and his entire scalp was gone. Both of the bandits in the trench were about forty years of age.

It became evident that Mr. Nevill had counted correctly, since we knew that five had escaped and twelve were dead. On the man who had jumped out of the trench, we found two bandoleers of .30-.30 ammunition and a .30-.30 rifle. He had been shot in at least ten places; one shot had taken off one of his ears. On this man we found Glenn's spurs and chaps. Because it was Mr. Nevill's wish that I keep them, I kept the chaps for twenty-five years.

We left the bandits where they had fallen and turned back to the river. Our horses simply had to have water. It was 4:30 in the afternoon. The horses had cooled down and were all dead tired, so we slipped their bridles and let them drink. All afternoon and even as he drank, my horse kept throwing his head around to the near side. I supposed he was wondering what kept stinging him. Later, I was able to work a bullet out of his flesh. As we watered the horses, we filled our canteens and drank, too, and we talked about poor Alberts' death, how lucky I had been, and how fortunate we were to be alive and not crippled.

Once again, the marksmanship of Mexicans had proven to be even worse than we thought possible. One thing that afternoon in our favor though, had been the fact that the bandits had to shoot sharply downhill. Still, it would be hard to imagine even very inexperienced American marksmen could fire over a hundred shots at that range without serious results. Yes, we were truly fortunate and with the exception of poor Alberts, not one of us had been scratched by a bullet.

While we were sitting in our saddles at the ford, the detail that had remained on the other bank with Alberts' body yelled a warning and then we heard yelling and shooting. We immediately rode out of the river without bridling our horses. We rode back about three hundred yards, and by that time, right down the ridge where they had made their first stand, came the five surviving bandits. The man on the snow-white horse—evidently the leader—had a rifle in his hands, and all of them were firing wildly. The distance between us was only about seven hundred yards, close enough to hear their curses. But their shots were falling short, and we even saw a few strike the riverbank. Our first volley, as we returned their fire, caused them to whirl and tear back up the ridge, but none appeared to be hit.

As we turned up the trail toward our headquarters, I don't believe any of us were very happy. It was sort of a funeral procession, as we had to wrap Alberts in blankets and tie him across his own horse. We knew his body would have to travel in that manner all of the fifty miles to Valentine, from where it would be shipped to his home by rail.

Our chase of the Nevill raiders had ended as we had hoped it might, except for the death of Alberts. A soldier has little choice in what he has to do, but we were all pretty sick of violent death. During the past five weeks we had seen enough for a lifetime. As it turned out, Nevill's raid was the very last one in the Big Bend.

Chapter 11—Justice in the Big Bend

I am quite sure that all of West Texas, and Jeff Davis and Presidio Counties in particular, knew of the unprovoked massacre at Porvenir, and they all must have known of the repercussions that followed, yet I doubt if any one has ever before read of the slaughter.

People today believe justice in the West was always being administered by some fearless, straight-shooting officer. The real situation will be a great shock and a terrible disappointment. In the events I am aware of, events that actually happened, the civil authorities provoked trouble instead of preventing it, and then ran for some place of safety—usually an inland town—and made what we all knew to be false reports, leaving the really dangerous and dirty work to be taken care of by the troop in whose jurisdiction the trouble had started. It was a shame all of the border trouble following the Columbus raid had been kept alive and growing by rumors, lies, and exaggerations.

Quiet investigations, which were believed to have originated in Austin, finally brought about a thorough housecleaning in Texas, by Texans, and it surely was about time.[50] In the aftermath of this period, some still considered it a joke to ambush four or five Mexicans, but whenever Mexicans retaliated, it was considered a terrible, cowardly crime. The newspapers responded to every killing of an American with loud, screaming publicity, but the killing of a Mexican was laughed off, regardless of whether he had ever been guilty of even a minor crime.

It was truly a sad time. Thirty-six Mexicans and four Americans were known to be dead as a result of the violence, and the ratio of ambushings stood, according to hearsay, at about twenty to one. After the raid, Mr. Nevill sold his cattle to a Mr. Spence of El Paso and moved his family to Marfa, where he opened the Longhorn Cafe on Main Street. It turned out to be the finest restaurant in Marfa. He later ran a café in Alpine, the closest town east of Marfa.

Naturally, there was a lot of talk about so many sudden deaths in the borderlands in so short a time. I believe it was Mr. Nevill who first said how much better justice would have been served if the four Rangers of the Porvenir incident had been tied on his porch the night of the raid—and believe me, all right-thinking people agreed with him—because anything the bandits might have done to them couldn't possibly have been as terrible as the crime the Rangers had committed themselves.

Porvenir and Pilares became ghost towns on the Texas side. The welcome sight of Luis Sánchez, the goat-herder and his wife with their gracious hospitality, was no more, and their sturdy two-room house was a shambles. Both of them were forced to flee for their lives into Chihuahua, leaving behind fifteen years' accumulation of personal property and over a thousand head of mohair goats.

When I returned to the Big Bend in 1963, the old adobe at the Upper Nevill Place was just about as I remembered. The pole corral where our horses had been stampeded by a mountain lion was still in good condition, but the windmill was gone. The Lower Nevill Ranch also looked about the same. Most of the water gaps from Mr. Nevill's day were in place, but badly in need of repair. Quail were still plentiful, but it seemed most of the wild burros and mules were gone, and all of the country was still uninhabited.

Chapter 12—Captain Matlack and the Aviators

In 1919, while I was still in the cavalry and before I joined the pack train as a civil servant, I transferred to K Troop at Captain Matlack's invitation, where I remained until my discharge in 1920. At the time of my transfer, I knew nothing about the river below Candelaria, where K Troop was camped, and new country had always fascinated me. The event I am now going to relate happened before my transfer, but Captain Matlack told me about it himself. Although Captain Matlack is no longer living, his only relative has given me permission to tell this story, which I deeply appreciate.

Operating out of Mexico at the time was the outlaw Chico Cano. Not long after Chico Cano visited Matlack in Candelaria, an incident took place involving the United States and Mexico in which Captain Matlack played the leading role and, I might add, a role that no one else cared to play.

Early one morning in August 1919, a message was delivered to Captain Matlack by a Mexican well known to the captain, from the little village across the river from Candelaria called San Antonio del Bravo. The note had been written by Lieutenant H. G. Peterson, an American aviator as they were called then, and it stated that he and his partner, Lieutenant Paul H. Davis, were prisoners of an outlaw called Orozco.

Leonard Matlack was the bravest man I have ever known. Everyone on the border knows of his deeds of outstanding bravery. Those of my old buddies whom I have been fortunate enough to see and talk to feel as sad over his death as I do. But never did I hear him brag about anything. It seemed natural for him to do a great many things that other men said were impossible.

He was just a shade better at shooting a pistol with his right hand than with his left, and he always carried two ivory handled .45 automatics. With his left hand he beat every man on the border who would ever shoot with him, so you have some idea of his value in tight places. Everyone who knew him remembers him, especially Lieutenants Davis and Peterson, who carried a warm place in their hearts for him because he rescued them from certain death.

Peterson and Davis, who were stationed at the small airfield at Lajitas, were flying a Jenny Scout plane, watching out for smugglers. On August 10, 1919, they left Lajitas on a bright, clear day. They had flown the mission many times, and were familiar with the area, and furthermore, they were carrying compasses and maps. But, within three hours, they made a forced landing near the Conchos River, twenty miles deep into Chihuahua, and although neither was hurt, the plane was wrecked.

The Conchos River is actually little more than a small stream that flows into the Rio Grande near Presidio. Its general direction is south to north while the Rio Grande flows west to east. The aviators flew twenty miles south with nothing but new, strange country under them, thinking they were still on the mighty Rio Grande. Both men said later that because they had become lost and confused, they had no idea they were in Mexico.

At the time they went down, the Conchos River was more like a dry stream than a river, but the two lieutenants claimed they had made a raft from logs and floated down the river until it was dusk. They camped on the bank of the river that night, they said, and continued their journey the following day. But that afternoon, they were approached by three Mexicans who gave them food and agreed to guide them to San Antonio, Chihuahua.

Everyone doubted the truth of their story. They should have asked to be taken to Ojinaga or Presidio, so they could reach Lajitas, instead of to San Antonio, which took them eighty miles out of their way. And how could they mistake the Conchos River for the Rio Grande? As the result of a navigation error, they said, they were captured by three Mexicans, Alfonso Quintanos, an old man, and his two boys.

Davis and Peterson both claimed that they had no idea where they were or even that they were, in any sense, prisoners. Yet the Mexicans were armed, and made the aviators walk ahead on the trail. All that day, August 11, they proceeded west in the direction of San Antonio, stopping from time to time to rest and eat tortillas.

Late in the afternoon, the party of five was met by three men riding horses. The two groups seemed to know each other, and the three horsemen were armed also. When the leader of the three, a man named Jesús Renteria who was missing part of an arm and a leg from a railroad accident in the U.S., threatened the other Mexicans with death if they didn't beat it, the prisoners were turned over to Renteria's gang. Their leader then threatened the two lieutenants with instant death if they tried to escape.[51]

According to the aviators, it was then that they began to suspect the Mexicans might ask for a reward, but they steadfastly maintained they never considered themselves prisoners. Renteria, however, instead of taking them to San Antonio del Bravo, took them to the hills west of the town and held them under heavy guard for a full week.

On the evening of August 17, the prisoners were brought down from the hills into San Antonio del Bravo, and entered the town after dark. They were taken to the home of Tómas Sánchez, where they spent the night. Sánchez was *presidente* of the town. Oddly enough, a scout for Matlack named Cabazula was there also.

Early in the morning of August 18, Tómas Sánchez crossed the river into Candelaria carrying a letter addressed to Dawkins Kilpatrick (a son of J. J. Kilpatrick, a local cotton grower and merchant of some reputation), who was at times engaged as a scout for Troop K. But instead of taking the letter he was carrying to Dawkins Kilpatrick, Sánchez brought it to the gate of our camp and asked to see Captain Matlack.

The note Sánchez delivered to Captain Matlack asked the Secretary of War, the families of the aviators, as well as their commanding officer, a Major Walton of El Paso, be notified; but the major message was that $10,000 in gold was to be paid to the bandits by midnight, August 20, or the aviators would be shot.

Many versions of this story traveled by rumor through the Big Bend. The *El Paso Times* of August 24, 1919, carried a large picture of Matlack with the caption: "Captain Matlack put Lieut. Davis on the back of his horse after Lieut. Davis was safe in United States territory, and rode off thumbing his nose at the Mexican Brigands, who demanded the unpaid half of the ransom money. 'I just told them to go to hell,' said Captain Matlack."

This was only one of many stories that circulated. The true story is just about as daring and exciting as any story can be, so why make such an intelligent man seem foolish? After Captain Matlack received the ransom demand, he immediately notified his superiors in Marfa and was assured the money would be sent to Candelaria. Matlack's second attempt to arrange the release of the prisoners for the payment of the ransom was successful. Here is the proposal, just as nearly as I can remember it:

"I, Captain Matlack, will come over on a sorrel horse and I will bring $5,000 and take one man back with me. Then I will return with $5,000 and take the other man back to Candelaria. The money will be in gold and I will be alone, and each time I will ride a sorrel horse so that you will know me. If these terms are not accepted, you can depend on this alternative: I will cross the river with a hundred men and we will kill everyone who harms or kills either of the men you are holding. Give the man who carries this message your answer quickly. I wish to start my first trip over by 3:00 p.m. this afternoon." And he signed it "Captain Leonard F. Matlack."

Orozco's answer, written by Lieutenant Peterson, said: "We accept your plan and the men will not be harmed if you carry out your part." It was signed "Orozco."

A man from the First National Bank of Marfa along with a major and other officers from the Eighth Cavalry brought the money down in two bank sacks. Matlack said that he understood the money for the ransom payment had been signed for by some wealthy cattlemen, who had been assured the government would make the money good. The incident attracted a huge amount of curious bystanders. Candelaria was overflowing with more people than had ever been there before, for any event. In the group were the Sheriff of Presidio County and all of his deputies, several Rangers, and the Ranger Captain from Marfa.

Previous stories have stated that the town was full of brave men. Maybe it was. Still, no one besides Matlack volunteered to ride that sorrel horse into the bandit hideout, about three miles south of the old San Antonio Trail. After Matlack was given one sack of money, he watched the point of a ridge with binoculars for the agreed signal—a fire. He started across the river on a sorrel horse toward the appointed spot.

He said that he rode at a lope, seeing no one, until he reached a narrow canyon where he was hailed by a Mexican who spoke some English. He was searched by the man, who held a pistol on him, and was asked if he had the money. Matlack only pointed to the bank sack and he was motioned into the canyon. In about a hundred yards, he was confronted by five armed Mexicans, and then Davis and Peterson moved out from behind some boulders.

Matlack said, "Who is Orozco?" and Davis pointed out the leader to him. "Then," Matlack told us, "I handed him the bank sack, and as two men guarded me, the other three counted.

"That," said the captain, "was the first time I had seen what was in the sack. Orozco seemed satisfied and in a hurry. He motioned Peterson to get on my horse."

During this time, Captain Matlack had not dismounted, so he nudged his horse over to a rock and helped the lieutenant up behind him and they left.

Matlack said to Davis, "I'll be back after you in a little while."

Peterson was not much of a rider, at least behind the cantle of a saddle, and it was quite a hard trip for him. As they rode, they talked. Peterson assured Matlack that they had been well fed and well treated since their capture. He told the captain the outlaws had both of their automatic pistols and four clips of ammunition, and that their plane was not badly damaged but was under guard about fifteen miles to the southwest.

When Matlack crossed back over the river, everybody wanted to ask questions, but he didn't stop until he and Peterson reached headquarters. Matlack's orderly was there with Big Red, his own private horse of the same color and very nearly a match in conformation to the one he was riding. Red was saddled and ready.

After giving a few orders regarding the care of Peterson, and telling his first lieutenant to have the troops ready to cross quickly if he did not return in two hours—it was then about an hour until sundown—he mounted and rode over to the man from the bank who had the rest of the money.

This time when he crossed the river, both of his ivory handled automatics were under his belt inside his shirt. He told us he definitely expected treachery on that trip, and one thing he was sure of, regardless of what happened, was they were not going to make him a prisoner.

"I know all about Mexican bandits," Matlack said. "This second trip, I loped Red back over the same trail. It was almost sundown when I met them all, a mile closer than they had been in the canyon. They were all riding horses, which I hadn't seen at all on the first trip.

"I smelled treachery even before Davis warned me with his eyes and by his manner. Two men were staying close to Orozco, and the other four started pulling slightly out to the sides. The expression on every face betrayed what was up. I figured they intended to take me, along with the money, and keep Davis, too, since this method of getting money had been so easy, up until then.

"All of these thoughts flashed through my mind in a second, as the two outside men moved out ten feet from Orozco. This situation had gone as far as I intended to allow it. Now every one of them looked at me with hate in their faces, but no word had been spoken at all, and no man had touched a gun.

"Orozco did speak to the man nearest to him, but in a low voice. I calculated the risk: seven guns against two. Instead of addressing me in a friendly manner, Orozco kept on talking in an undertone to the man next to him. My shirt was unbuttoned, and I moved my hand like I was going to pat Red on the neck. Instead I came out with one .45.

"Every man of them froze for an instant, which gave me time to come out with the other .45. In the second all of this took, I yelled to Davis, 'Come here!' and he never hesitated, but when he moved at my yell Orozco yelled, *'Maten a los Gringos!'*—'Kill the Americans!'

"When the first shot was fired, old Red never moved an ear, but the Mexican's horses went wild, and so did their shots. With only thirty feet separating us, I yelled at Davis to stay behind Red. Although I had only three shells left in each gun, three of the bandits broke and ran, spurring and lashing their horses. One got clear away. I slipped extra clips into the guns and dropped one of the empties on the ground accidentally.

"Then I kneed Red over to a rock and Davis got up behind me. He said, 'God, man, I never thought you could do it. I was sure they would kill us both. I never saw anything like it. It didn't seem possible.'

"We left there at a fast gallop and kept it up all the way to the river. It was pretty dark by the time I crossed the ford at Lower San Antone.

"I had no intention of doing what I was forced to do that evening, even if Davis had not warned me, and he did warn me with his eyes, just as certainly as he told me on the way back, 'They talked of nothing after you left with Peterson, but how to get the rest of the money, and how to hold us both or to kill us if they had to. It never entered their heads that you'd make a fight. I understood enough of their lingo to know they had nothing but contempt for you, but knowing that you were a captain, they figured you would bring even more money.'

"Candelaria was full of people, as you know," Captain Matlack told me, "but I talked to no one except my superior officer from Regimental Headquarters and the man from the bank, to whom I returned the rest of the money. A captain and several Rangers were present and over a hundred civilians from all over the country. They all wanted to know what happened, but I told them nothing.

"I was starved and so were Peterson and Davis, and we ate enough for ten men. The next morning I took the troop over at daylight and scouted all day. We never saw a living bandit or anyone else, but we found a few trinkets.

"I was criticized by higher officers at first, but never by Colonel Langhorne. Later, when I explained what I had been forced to do and Lieutenant Davis confirmed my story, there was no more criticism. Everybody apologized, commended my action, and informed me that I was a brave man.

"I never learned who came into all the gold that was paid over for Peterson, but some bandit, perhaps, retired."

★ ★ ★

From the beginning, erroneous stories circulated which conflicted with what Captain Matlack told us, but no one else could have known the truth. In the beginning, Matlack was expected to keep the word of the United States by returning the balance of the money to the bandit leader, but it was impossible to deliver the money, because there was no bandit leader left. The other members of the gang were Slim Olivas and Juan Maravette. So Matlack returned the money to the ranchers of Marfa who had offered it for the ransom.

Captain Matlack told very few of this astounding incident in his life. He seldom ever mentioned it, but for sheer cool-headed bravery, I know of no other true story that can equal it. Had it been many men against such odds, they could have made a safe getaway, but what would have happened to Davis? Red was a real quarter horse and could have carried the captain to safety in a few mighty leaps, but running away from danger was not a part of Matty's makeup. It is easy to understand why K Troop was always proud of their captain.

I had seen Captain Matlack in a tight spot. He was not only cool-headed, but he also inspired confidence in anyone near him. He was the kind of a man that would set an example that could turn a coward into a hero. On many occasions I have watched him shoot at two targets with a .45 in each hand. At a hundred feet, using a six-inch bull's eye and shooting rapidly, he just never missed. Naturally, he alternated, first left, and then right. He was one of the few real two-handed gunmen who ever lived.

After the ransoming, a tragic accident befell the three gang members. As they were heading for Coyame, an American scouting plane from Lajitas, out early, saw the three horsemen and fired on them although the plane was five miles off course, and flying over Mexico. The first volley knocked Renteria and his horse down, going through his cork leg, killing the horse, and pinning Renteria under it. The two other gang members escaped into a brushy canyon.

Some believed Renteria wasn't hurt, but that he had great difficulty getting out from under his horse. One story said he walked a while and then hailed a man riding a burro. He bought the burro and rode it back to San Antonio, transferred his old saddle to a new horse, and made his getaway.

This affair of the rescue of Peterson and Davis from bandits in Mexico was investigated by a Senate Investigating Committee in El Paso in 1920. Senator Albert B. Fall (later Secretary of the Interior) served as Chairman of the Committee. Matlack was interrogated about his part, and when the facts were laid before the committee, they offered Matlack nothing but praise. He was completely exonerated, as he should have been.

Following this incident, the Commanding General of the Big Bend Military District ordered a Punitive Expedition, consisting of three hundred cavalrymen, a pack train, and ten scouts to invade Chihuahua and to find and annihilate Renteria and his gang. It was about forty hours before any action was decided on and the expedition was wild, erratic, and confused. But even at that late date, ten men would have had a 50–50 chance of success, but three hundred had no chance whatever. It is such judgments that lose men and battles needlessly.

A Major Yancey, who knew nothing of the country or the circumstances, was sent down to the river to take command of the Second Punitive Expedition in border history. I was grateful my old Troop G was left to patrol the one hundred miles of the river while the Punitive Expedition searched for Renteria in Mexico.

The troops passed by San Antonio del Bravo, where a careful inquiry should have been made and where all information should have been available. It would have been helpful to know what color horses they were riding, whether they were shod, and from what corral they had left. It would also have been helpful to know the brand on their horses, whether the men carried food, if they were armed, and if so, what kind of weapons they carried. And most important, in which direction had they headed and how long had they been gone.

Apparently, the major even ignored the information offered by the scouts, who knew exactly what kind of country they were in. After they arrived at Coyame, the major was at a loss as to what to do next. He had a description of Renteria, but he wouldn't have known the others if he had seen them.

We camped that night near a large dirt tank with a good windmill and an abundance of water. We were no less than twenty miles as the crow flies from the main body of troops, but there was a good-sized mountain range between us. Several hundred Carranza troops had passed through the previous day, and the natives thought we were trailing them. There had been little friendship shown by anyone, and we had an uncomfortable feeling about being in a country where we had no legitimate business.

The expedition spent four days in Mexico without making any effort to catch Renteria. Four Mexican prisoners were killed near Corrizo Springs by three of the civilian scouts during an escape attempt. Of the four, three had good reputations and the fourth had been accused of murder but not indicted. As a result of the deaths, and of false reporting, Major Yancey was court-martialed and given a light sentence: six months' suspension and a fine.[52]

On the evening of the third day of the Expedition, our troops were visited by a Carranza colonel along with two hundred well-mounted cavalry. An educated and courteous man, he demanded an explanation for the presence of such a large force of U.S. Cavalry in his country. The major explained about the capture of the aviators. But when the colonel asked for a description of the bandits, only the scout Cabazula came to his aid. The colonel told the major he would take care of the bandits, and that the Expedition must return to the border within twenty-four hours.

The Candelaria incident, when a hidden ambusher attempted to murder the two Kilpatricks, was the last event of any consequence that occurred during my time on the border. By the close of 1919, Carranza had a good grip on the situation. Between the regular Carranza troops stationed at all of the strategic points along the border; and the Rurales, who had been reorganized for the first time since Chief Kosterlitzsky left Mexico in 1913, bandits and outlaws were being apprehended, and the entire length of the border was quiet.

Addendum—The Pack Train

By 1920, all fourteen government pack trains were under the Civil Service. During the Mexican Revolution, and until 1922, there were two pack trains in the Big Bend, Army Pack Train One and Army Pack Train Two. Pack trains had always fascinated me and I felt I would be happy when I left the cavalry if I could land a job as a packer. Jimmy Everett,[53] my best friend in the Big Bend and a native of Valentine, was a packer on Army Pack Train Two. He took me out to their camp at the Holland Ranch, and introduced me to his pack master, Charley Coward. When Charley hired me, Jimmy became my instructor and partner. He was a Texan who lived there thirty-five years, spoke fluent Mexican,[54] and knew what went on down there perhaps better than any other man. He is one of the smoothest riders I have ever known, and a good roper and bronco rider, too.

We were paid in gold by the Army Paymaster, $100 per month, and everything was furnished except our clothing. The Army even had a good stock saddle, but both Jimmy and I had ours custom made by a man named Myers in El Paso.

When Jimmy and I worked as partners, each weighing around 160 pounds, no two packers on any of the trains ever beat us at anything. We had ten mules to rig, load, and take care of on the trail, and everything we did was carried out in a competitive manner. We raced to rig out our mules first, manta our share of the cargo first, sling our loads first, and throw the diamond hitch, which secured the loads on the mule's back, first.[55] It was heavy, hard work, but we loved it, and although we were forty pounds lighter than any of the other packers, no matter how fast they threw those 150 pound loads, we could match any crew.

Charley Coward, our pack master, had been at it for over forty years, and he swore that he would bet a year's pay we could beat any two packers in the world, but Charley always swore about something. I have never worked at any other job where hard work was play or where such a competitive spirit prevailed among men. Those who have never seen a heavily loaded fifty-mule train on the trail, with their white canvas loads held by a beautiful diamond hitch, have missed a thrilling spectacle.

In Pack Train Two there were fifty pack mules, fourteen saddle mules, and a bell mare, as well as ten packers, a cook, a blacksmith, and a *cargador* or mule-shoer, besides the pack master.

Government oats weighing an average of 160 pounds to the sack constituted the heaviest loads we carried. The average a pack mule could carry was two 150-pound loads and with a full train, we carried more than fourteen thousand pounds of cargo, going anywhere that deer normally ran.

A packer and his partner had twelve mules to look after: ten pack mules and their two saddle mules. We usually worked every other day. On work mornings, we would go to the corral and rig out the train around 4:00 a.m. This job consisted of seeing that the mule's back was clean, and placing a properly folded woolen blanket on the mule's back, then the rigging, or *aparejo,* which had a breeching. This was the finest type of rigging ever devised to carry heavy loads and give a minimum of trouble to both the mule's back and the packer.

"Rigging out the train" was similar to saddling several horses, except that we used an eight-inch canvas cinch, with heavy rings and a six-foot *latigo* strap with which you could securely tie the rig. This was called "Killing the Mule," and a bystander would have thought the mule was actually being killed by the way he would grunt and groan.

The cargo we carried each trip was prepared the previous evening and covered with a special canvas, just as the riggings were when not in use. The two loads each mule carried had been wrapped in heavy canvas and securely lashed, one placed on top of the other. The canvas manta was of the highest quality and six-feet square. After the material we were packing was placed in the center of the manta, the four corners would be folded over tightly. An important part of preparing the loads was to make them of equal weight.

Lashing the load came next with a "lair" rope thirty feet long and three-eighths inches thick. It had a loop in one end, just as a cowboy's catch rope did. The packer widened the loop, placed it around the load the long way, and drew it tight, then threw an overhand half-hitch around the load the narrow way, and then another, drawing both tight. Holding the slack, the packer next threw an underhand half-hitch around the end close to him, drawing it tight, securing the end of the rope in a bowknot that one jerk could loosen. After that, the load was ready.

After the full train was rigged out, we went to the cook-shack, where the cook had a hearty breakfast ready for us. On those days, it would be the only hot meal of the day. When we finished breakfast, we would go back to the corral and load out.

When we were ready to load out, the mule was caught by the halter, which they always wore, and blindfolded. A mule never moved as long as he was blindfolded. Next, a thirty-foot "sling" rope, also three-eighths inches, was thrown across the rigging by the near-side man, keeping the loop, or doubled part, next to him while the two loose ends would be on the off side. Each man would then jerk his load from the ground and, using his knee, toss the rope high on the rigging and hold it in place with his elbow. Jimmy worked the near side of the mule, the side on the right as you faced the mule, while I worked the off side, on the left.

Both of the loads would initially be tied together, high in the center of the rigging. Then the off-side man, with his right hand, grabbed the end of the front rope and tossed it across to the near-side man, who tied it into the front part of the loop using a double bowknot. Next, the rear end was thrown across and tied in the same manner.

The packer then had the loads slung on the mule's rigging and they were shaken and pulled until they balanced. However, the final test of balance was made by putting a finger under the corner of the lower part of the rigging itself. If it rocked at the touch and then settled back to normal, it was perfectly equalized.

Next came the "lash" rope, with which the diamond hitch was formed. This rope was actually two twenty-five foot ropes, one-half inch thick, skillfully spliced together. Braided into one end of this rope was a canvas cinch five inches in width and five feet in length, with a brass hook riveted into the cinch at the other end. Over all, the lash rope was fifty-five feet long.

The near-side man started the diamond hitch by passing the cinch with the brass hook attached under the mule's belly. The off-side man caught the hook. This operation was performed with the near-side man's right foot, while he caught the rope about ten feet from the cinch, formed a large loop, and threw it across the top of the load with his hands. The off-side man caught the loop and placed it in the brass hook.

While this was going on, the near-side man was forming his part of the diamond hitch and grasping one side of the loop he had just thrown across the top of the load. He would then yell "Kill the Mule," indicating to his partner that he was ready to hold the slack, as the off-side man began cinching the rope tight through the hook while the near-side man held every bit of it. With a knee against the mule, he pulled the rope as tight as he could with his partner holding the slack. Then it was his turn, and he first pulled the slack from the rear rope at the *aparejo* corner. Two ropes crossed the load's middle and one crossed each corner. When done, all ropes would fairly sing, they were so tight.

Then one of the packers would jerk off the blindfold and the mule would go grunting off toward the bell mare. The bell mare is vital to a train of mules, for without the bell mare, it would be almost impossible to hit the trail. There would surely be confusion and perhaps damage. Every pack mule I ever worked with grunted and groaned something awful when they were first turned loose. Some soon quit complaining, while others grunted every step of the trip, even if it happened to be fifty or sixty miles.

When all the mules were packed, the pack master, who did nothing except put the saddle on his own mule, would start off leading the bell mare and the fifty-mule pack train started on its journey. You may be sure it was always somewhere that even a jeep couldn't possibly go. The pack master set a pace of about six miles an hour and he never looked back, or stopped, except on very rare occasions.

If the trip was an overnight affair, the cook would accompany us, in place directly behind the pack master on the trail, and when he traveled with us, it was he who led the bell mare. The train actually went in five sections. Directly behind the cook and bell mare came ten loaded mules, followed by the two partners who were responsible for them, then ten more mules and two packers until all sixty-five animals were strung out.

At the very rear came the mule-shoer (or blacksmith) and the *cargador*, whose duty on the trail was to watch for mules that might have lost a shoe. When that happened, the train was usually stopped, but it rarely happened. In camp, the *cargador* doctored mules that developed small sores on their backs, but that too was rare, since every rigging was a double-prime cowhide, inside of which we placed green willow reeds in a vertical position, and between the reeds and the mule's sides and back, we stuffed soft Timothy hay.

Each mule had his or her private rigging which had been perfectly fitted to the animal's back by cinching it on while the willows were green and pliable and allowing it to set to the mule's individual back. On the inside half of the rigging there was a round hole big enough to put your hand in. If there happened to be too much pressure in one spot, causing a sore, the packer could simply pull the hay away from that spot, and no weight would then rest on the sore. I have seen bad sores healed while the mule carried a load every day, with the *cargador* using nothing but a carbolic soap solution applied with a sponge. The *cargador* was the only man in the Big Bend whom I couldn't beat at the time I was in the pack train.

There was no item we didn't pack on a mule. One time we packed a cook stove from Valentine to Evetts Ranch. For the greater part of the time, though, the cargos were canned goods, flour, sugar, baled hay, and oats. Gasoline barrels, cook stoves, and bailed hay were the most difficult of all loads to keep straight on a mule's back. Since most of the packing was done over narrow Indian trails with large rocks and tree limbs at the side to knock the wide loads crooked, any packer with heavily loaded mules had, at each moment, a challenge on his hands.

If a load became crooked in your group of ten mules, it was time for action. Each packer carried a specially constructed blindfold, usually over his shoulder. Jimmy and I would ride up to the mule with the crooked load, much in the manner of bulldoggers today, one on each side of the animal. Once in front of him, we would turn our mules together, jump off on the run, and have him blindfolded in no time at all. Our saddle mules were trained to stand all day if necessary. After the mule was blindfolded, the diamond hitch would be loosened by jerking one double bowknot. Then we would re-balance the load and pull the hitch tight again.

This was where Jimmy and I were by far the fastest of all. Speed was necessary in straightening a crooked load. If we didn't work fast, the entire train would go by us, and the mule would have to gallop all of the way until it found its place in the train, and chances are, the load would be crooked again. Jimmy and I could usually perform the stunt in about thirty seconds, and the mule could take its place most of the time without running at all. After we jerked the blindfold, we practiced getting on our mules on the fly. I was never as good at this as Jimmy, but the older men in the train thought we were a pair of show-offs. We were about twenty, but Jimmy could still run a hundred yards in ten seconds after he was forty years old.

My mule, Buckshot, was small, probably weighing less than nine hundred pounds, but he was fast and quick as a cat. After he had packed all day, he could still throw me if I got careless. Riding him, I could catch a mule with a crooked load so quickly that I would lose my hat unless I pulled it down beforehand. He always knew which mule I wanted, and would put me up in front of him, so all I had to do was start to lean to the near side for Buckshot to slide to a stop like a baseball player, with his hind feet right up to the front ones. I would hang on by the saddle horn with my feet touching the ground. We could catch and blindfold the mule almost before he knew we were after him. We practiced sliding stops from a dead run, and getting on and off in the same manner. Jimmy and I were the only packers who did this, but we were young, strong men and thoroughly enjoyed it, and I am damn sure the mules we rode did, too.

Buckshot was a wonderful saddle animal, and in the mountains I would rather have ridden him than any of the fine, sure-footed horses I have been fortunate enough to ride. As most mules do, though, Buckshot had one bad trait, the studs.[56] He would do everything asked of him just as long as he was inside the pack train, but on other occasions he drove me crazy. I could have won a million dollars with him by betting anybody any amount of money they couldn't ride him anywhere he didn't want to go. A part of the bet would have been that he wouldn't buck, balk, lie down, or rear up, either.

No animal on earth, not even a camel, could make a man feel as foolish as a mule with the studs. Many times I tried to ride him to Valentine alone, and just as long as he didn't hear the bell mare, he went off at a nice lope for maybe as far as half a mile, but when he heard that bell tinkle, I had had it. He wouldn't try to run off, or even turn his head in the direction of the train, but he would stop, wring his tail, and squeal and kick as hard as he could with both hind feet. With every kick he would still be headed toward Valentine, but his tail would be six feet closer to that bell mare, and so would I. Buckshot would always stop of his own accord, but when he did so he would be broadside of the corral gate with me sitting in the saddle, feeling and looking like a fool. Any man who ever worked in a pack train knows what it means to "kill the mule," and although the term refers to the task of cinching the rigging on tight when a mule is fighting it by swelling up, Buckshot surely made me want to apply it in another way.

Our toughest packing was done between Marfa and Presidio, a distance of sixty miles. The best mare mules carried about 320 pounds, and made the trip in nine hours without a stop. In all of my time in the pack train, only two mules ever fell while carrying a load, and both times it was on that terrible jumping off place above Shafter, where the silver mines are located, a short distance from Presidio, Texas.[57] Both times the mule had to be unloaded before she could get to her feet.

Of all occupations, I would be willing to bet that every man who ever worked on a pack train regretted the day the government decided to abolish them. Every packer loved the work, although it was strenuous and even dangerous at times. The average weight of the mules was about 1,050 pounds, but the very best pack mule in our train was a mare that weighed a thousand pounds. The train never lost a mule or cargo. A great deal can be said of the ability of the men who used to pack mules for the train service. I was never afraid of the mules, and was never hurt by one and neither, to my knowledge, was Jimmy, but we had one man we called Swede in the train who was kicked almost daily. He swore he had been kicked by a mule at a distance of twenty feet.

Charley Coward was a master of mules. No one knew his secret, if there was one, but I always thought it was the tone of his deep voice. No mule ever so much as kicked at him, and when Swede or someone else got kicked, and Charley heard of it, he would walk right up behind the mule and kick the mule real hard, high on the tail. Don't ask me why the mules didn't wallop him when he walked behind them, no one ever figured that out, but just as he turned loose with that number ten of his, he would always say in his deep gruff voice, "What's the mater with Yu?" Well, I watched him kick most of them, and all they ever did was look surprised, tremble violently, and by the time his voice quit ringing, the mule would be squatting so low, its belly would almost touch the ground.

While I am on the subject of the pack train, I might as well tell of an experience Jimmy and I had at Marfa. When we were at the foot of the Viejo Trail, in camp at the Holland Ranch, all of the mules except a couple of the saddle animals were turned into a two-section pasture to graze between trips. When we camped at Marfa and packed to Presidio, there was no fenced pasture, so each packer and his partner took turns herding the sixty-two mules on open range.

Well, Jimmy and I were on that job one day, and it was a job none of us cared for. This particular day, Jimmy and I were sitting on our mules, each with a leg across the saddle horn, talking, when all at once all sixty-two mules started braying and took off in a dead run. We could see they were after a small burro, which was running toward the camp at Marfa. Mules are crazy over colts and small burros, sometimes actually killing them with love and affection after running them down. We never gained an inch in that two-mile race, coming in sixty-third and sixty-fourth.

At Marfa, even the officers' quarters were tents, but they had board floors, and board sides reaching up four feet from the floors. Those field tents were stretched over the frame from a ridge, or center pole, and the tent ropes secured to stakes for additional strength. There were six rows of tents altogether, each over a half-mile in length, and several other structures, but for the most part the other buildings were wooden—the canteen for example.

That lousy burro belonged to some officer's children, and he was heading for home. It was a serious situation, all right, but we had to laugh, I'll tell you. It seemed incredible that so small an animal could outrun those big mules, but he did, all the way to camp. However, at the third tent he ducked in beside it, and all of the mules that could make the turn did so, and down went a tent. Well, sir, that burro nearly got caught then, but he never stopped running, on through that bunch of tents, until finally he was forced to take off again toward town. In one tent, a hot poker game was in progress. Looks of pure hatred followed me and Jimmy as we went flying by, lying low on our mules' necks and laying on the leather.

Down near the reservation gate was a five-strand barbed wire fence, and that burro never even slowed up for it. Somehow he got through in one piece, but the wire fence ended the race because, crazy as mules are about a few things, a wire fence doesn't happen to be one of them. It would be impossible to run a mule through one, day or night. The crazy things stood there and brayed and bellered, though, like they had lost a relative.

You can imagine how Jimmy and I felt when we had to face everybody at camp. They all wanted to kill us, but I swore we had done our best, although it wasn't nearly good enough. In addition to the destruction of property and a couple of mules going lame—having been crowded into something, I suppose—Charley threatened to fire us, and even the other packers, who had no call whatever to stick their noses into it, acted as if the damned mules had run them over.

That was one Big Bend event that needed no exaggeration, and as Jimmy and I have always said: Just think what the outcome would have been if one of those screaming Mexican bandits had been riding each of those mules and succeeded in reaching the city of Marfa! We were all under the jurisdiction of the Acting Regimental Commander, who at the time was Major Bentley, I believe, and the mule stampede had one bright aftermath: we stopped herding the pack train mules. From that day on, they had to be satisfied with baled hay.

Jimmy and I always believed someone had hauled that burro out there in a car or truck, someone who knew how crazy mules are over such an animal. Jimmy and I loved this work. We could manta-up a mule's cargo ready to load in less than ten seconds. We loved to beat the other pairs of packers who were all highly competitive. And although he never let on, we knew that Charley Coward, the pack master, liked our work very much. After the wild burro chase, Charley bawled us out and said he could have turned the mules, but later on, he relented and had a good laugh every time he looked at us.

Notes

Editor's Introduction

1. Cecelia Thompson, *History of Marfa and Presidio County, Volume Two, 1901–1946* (Austin: Nortex Press, 1985), 97. "There was some question about the extent of Chico Cano's villainy. There were implications that he was framed by ambitious military officers who gained publicity at his expense." Also, for another lucid account which focuses on the raids, see Glenn Justice, *Revolution on the Rio Grande: Mexican Raids and Army Pursuits, 1916–1919* (El Paso: Texas Western Press, 1992).

2. Thompson, 100.

3. Thompson, 100.

4. Thompson, 102–103.

5. Thompson, 115.

6. The military encampment at Marfa was referred to by various names, including Camp Marfa, until it was formally designated a military post under the name Fort D. A. Russell in 1929. Thompson, 136.

7. In his book, *Anglos and Mexicans in the Making of Texas 1836–1986* (Austin: University of Texas Press, 1987), David Montejano proposes that the original, more civilized relations between Mexicans and Anglos were damaged by the transition from the old ranching economy into an agricultural economy which "expressed itself in bitter political contests between 'old-timer' ranchers and 'newcomer' farmers," 9. This analysis was more appropriate to the eastern border and the valley than to the Big Bend. However, Montejano also refers directly to the "repression carried out by the Texas Rangers," 105, saying that there was a decline of the previously "friendly feelings which had slowly developed between the old American and Mexican families," 114. These feelings, he claims, had been replaced by a "feeling of hate, distrust and jealousy on the part of the Mexicans," 115, due to the decline of respect paid them by Anglos. The author refers to old-time attorney Frank Pierce, who claimed that many killings took place when Mexicans were placed under arrest, and to Emelio Forto, Cameron County Sheriff, who

added that "'a large share of the border troubles could be explained by the reckless manner in which undisciplined 'pistol toters' have been permitted to act as trial judge, jury, and executioners.'" 116.

Montejano echoes Keil's comments on the origins of border violence by quoting P. S. Taylor as saying, "'in many revolutionary situations, vengeance for specific wrongs rather than commitment to a radical ideology was the prime catalyst behind the Texas Mexican insurrection.'" The overall situation was tragic. "Mexicans with whom they [the Anglos] had lived in harmony for years avoided contact. Mexicans who had always been tractable and friendly became sullen." 119. P. S. Taylor, *An American-Mexican Frontier: Nueces County, Texas* (Chapel Hill: University of North Carolina Press, 1934; reprint, New York: Russell and Russell, 1971).

He describes the Texas Rangers as in cooperation with land speculators, having killed "between 500 and 5000 Mexicans" in the valley, 125, and "massacred hundreds of unarmed, peaceful Mexican villagers and seized their lands." 127. He also points out that "Even Webb, the Ranger historian, acknowledged that 'many innocent Mexicans were made to suffer' and that 'many members of the force have been heartily ashamed of their part in the orgy of bloodshed.'" 127.

At the beginning of Part Two, "Reconstruction," Montejano, 103, quotes a Texas Ranger Patrol Song, circa 1900:

> O bury me not on the lone praire-ee
> Where the wild coyotes will howl o'er me
> In a narrow grave just six by three
> Where all the Mexkins ought to be-ee!

8. Thompson, 116.
9. Thompson, 123.
10. Gerald G. Raun, "The National Guard on the Border and One Soldier's Viewpoint," *Journal of Big Bend Studies* 6 (1994): 129.
11. Raun, 124.
12. Arthur R. Gómez, "The Glen Springs-Boquillas Raid Reconsidered: Diplomatic Intrigue on the Rio Grande," *Journal of Big Bend Studies* 4 (1992): 97.
13. Thompson, 127.
14. Thompson, 127.
15. Thompson, 127.

16. Gómez, 102–103.

17. Thompson, 132.

18. Thompson, 132.

19. W. D. Smithers, *Chronicles of the Big Bend* (Austin: Madrona Press, Inc., 1976), 197.

20. Gómez, 104–105.

21. Gómez, 107.

22. Gómez, 110.

23. Joyce Means, *Pancho Villa Days at Pilares,* rev. ed. (Tucson, Az. [306 W. President St., Tucson 85714], 1994). This book, rich with anecdotes, dates, and names, is essentially a written version of oral history, and includes all the variations Means could find to any story that interested her. But although it includes contradictory accounts, it also confirms, in many instances, the material in other sources.

Chapter 2

24. The word "bosque" as used in this manuscript refers to the small Mexican-American settlement of Bosque Bonito, but in a larger sense, to the area along the Rio Grande on both sides, and specifically the U.S. side, whose vegetation typically consists of wooded scrub thickets, reeds, chino grama, leatherstem, willows, mesquite, cottonwood, and catclaw. The reeds, desert willows, and saltcedars give it a dreamy appearance, but in fact, the presence of thorned vegetation makes it a difficult hiding place. See: Barton H. Warnock, *Wildflowers of the Big Bend Country* (Alpine, Tx: Sul Ross State University, 1970), Fig. 3.

25. The javelina is a spotted peccary related to the wild hog. Because of a gland near the tail that gives off a strong odor when the animal is excited, it is sometimes called "musk hog." Javelinas travel in packs and can become vicious when cornered.

26. The United States census reports for Presidio County indicate that the county population in 1900 was approximately 379, including three members of the Brite family and one servant. The 1910 census numbers only 258, but includes three members of the Neill family, who worked for the Brite Ranch. It also includes the large José (Luis) Sánchez family, the goat herders, as well as the eight members of the Sitters family and five members of the Castillo family, who worked for Ed Nevill. Generally, the younger Castillo children lived with Rosa Castillo's mother. The population had declined by about a third between 1900 and 1910. The 1920 census shows a large increase to 542, including only one Brite, Charles, the Evetts (three family members), and a number of

families who were apparently new to the area, perhaps some being refugees from the revolution in Mexico.

27. Bosque Bonito is located about thirty-five miles south of Sierra Blanca, Texas. There was a wagon road that went from there to the famous T.O. Ranch, and then on to Chihuahua City, Mexico. It was a convenient place to bring out stolen cattle from Mexico. Robert Keil wrote to a friend that the *El Paso Times* had an article on the T.O. Ranch on June 18, 1925.

Chapter 3

28. The number seems excessive; however, raids were apparently sometimes made from Mexico into Texas by Federalist and revolutionary soldiers. For example, one of the bandits at the Brite raid was dressed "in the uniform of a Carranza officer." Thompson, 148.

29. There was so much cattle and horse thievery during those years in the borderland that it is tempting to attribute the motivation for some of the raids to a simple need for livestock—horses to ride and cattle to eat.

30. Mike Cox, *Texas Ranger Tales II* (Plano, Tx: Republic of Texas Press, 1999), 164–169. Even this book, put together by former Rangers, insinuates that the actions of the Rangers could have been questionable.

Chapter 4

31. Camp Marfa, later known as Fort D. A. Russell.

32. The "San Antone" Trail ran from Porvenir downriver to Boquillas Canyon on the American side, and from Pilares to Ojinaga on the Mexican side before turning south into Chihuahua, Mexico. For a clear map of the trail, see Smithers, inside cover.

33. The *Texas Almanac of 2000–2001* (Mary G. Ramos, ed., Dallas: The Dallas Morning News, 1999), carries a history of the Texas Rangers that claimed they and other vigilantes had killed between 300 and 5,000 Mexicans between 1910 and 1919. The history refers to a Legislative investigation of the Rangers by José T. Canales of Brownsville that led to the passing of legislation on March 31, 1919, which reduced the number of Rangers while raising their pay in an attempt to attract higher quality men. See 26. There is little doubt, however, that part of the problem was the job description, beginning in 1917 and continuing until the early 1930s, included "town taming."

34. There is some confusion in the names of the towns Porvenir and Pilares. The map in Smithers' book places Porvenir on the Texas side and Pilares directly across the Rio

Grande on the Mexican side. Other sources have given the name of Pilares to both towns, or claimed that the name of Pilares (Texas side) was later changed to Porvenir.

35. This version of the Keil manuscript was dated 1959.

Chapter 5

36. In some documents, the name was spelled Welch. It was generally supposed that the bandit who cut Welsh's throat was Jesús Renteria. Means, 186.

37. It was speculated that the bandits were diverted and the family's lives were saved when Sam Neill gave up the key to the Brite store at Mrs. Neill's insistence. Thompson, 146.

Chapter 6

38. This number seems unlikely considering that in one of the fiercest battles of the Revolution, in Ojinaga on January 10, 1914, the Federalist army Villa defeated was made up of only five thousand, including women, children, and camp followers. Ronald Atkin, *Revolution! Mexico 1910–1920* (New York: The John Day Company, 1970), 168.

Chapter 8

39. It was generally believed by the Rangers that Chico Cano, who was frequently around Pilares or Porvenir, was the instigator of the Brite raid and was responsible for the theft of forty to fifty horses. Many believe that Jesús Renteria was at the site. Means, 187–188. When Captain J. M. Fox of the Texas Rangers heard that the people of Porvenir seemed to have new clothing, he assumed it had been stolen from the Brite commissary during the raid there. However, an alternate story is that Ed Nevill had purchased the clothing and given it to the people of Porvenir. Some believed that Villa went on the Brite raid, and others that Placido Villanueva had ordered it and was executed by Villa in reprisal. According to *Texas Ranger Tales II,* Captain Fox had joined the Rangers on October 5, 1911, and had been appointed on the same day to the position of Captain by Governor Oscar B. Colquitt, 163. He thus had no experience to prepare him for his responsibility. According to Means, after the Porvenir raid, Brite would not allow a Ranger on his land. Means, 189.

40. This view of Anglo-Mexican relations is simplistic but not entirely inaccurate.

41. Perhaps some of the confusion over the names of Pilares and Porvenir arises from the very small and transient populations in the border towns, as well as the fragile and ephemeral nature of their housing.

Chapter 9

42. Joyce Means refers to the Castillos as Clara and Adrian, and quotes José Castillo as referring to his mother as Clara, 203. The 1910 census lists a Castillo family including Avarado, Cista, Ardriano, Clara, and José. No Castillos appear on the 1920 census.

43. The Nevill children were Glenn, who lived at the ranch with his father, and Grace, Tom, Lois, and Edith, who lived in town with their mother, presumably to attend school. Lois later changed the spelling of the name from Nevill to Neville. This information is available in the papers of the Dr. Clifford B. Casey Collection, Box 5, File 468, Archives of the Big Bend, Sul Ross State University.

44. Means, 203.

45. To cut for sign means to check the environment for evidence of the presence or passage of men or animals.

46. There were a number of theories about the cause of the Nevill raid. Keil clearly believed it was in revenge for the Porvenir massacre. However, Means noted that Villa had recently asked Nevill for horses and been refused, 211, and José later reported that the raiders took all the horses, 211. An oral history by Enrique Madrid of Redford, Texas, tells the story of a man who came into his mother's library in the 1980s and claimed that Rosa was killed for turning in illegal immigrants, and that her death was the real purpose of the raid. Others claim that Rosa was killed because she could identify the raiders. Means, 209. José Castillo later said, "My mother, Clara, was accidentally killed. She was not disfigured as some reported." 211. There were some who reported there was a second Mexican family living at the Nevill Ranch, although not necessarily at the same time, and that the workers had a grievance against Rosa. (Personal communitcation from Joyce Means.) Some timelines actually place the Nevill raid *before* the Porvenir massacre. Like so many other things that happened in those years on the border, with no reliable reporting, and so much storytelling, the real reasons for the raid may never be discovered.

47. Compressed cottonseed was used in large pellets (smaller than a fist) to feed cattle.

48. Thompson reports that E. W. Nevill testified "on the witness stand before U.S. Senate Subcommittee hearings in El Paso, February 3, 1920, that on March 25, 1918, his house was raided by Mexicans and shot full of holes, and his son and housekeeper were killed." Nevill told how he escaped and hid in a ditch, but "his son was caught in the house and shot to pieces . . ." Thompson, 151–152.

Chapter 10

49. The "Hot Pursuit Treaty" between the U.S. and Mexico provided permission for law enforcement officers pursuing a criminal to cross the national boundary.

Chapter 11

50. At the instigation of J. J. Kilpatrick, Sr. of Candelaria, who started a cotton empire there, an investigation of the aviator incident was conducted by the U.S. Senate and led by Senator Albert Fall in December 1919 and well into 1920. Thompson, 179. A letter from Colonel George T. Langhorne, stating that the money for the ransom of the two aviators had been obtained from Marfa ranchers, cleared Captain Leonard Matlack from any suspicion of wrongdoing in failing to pay the entire ransom to the bandits and returning the remainder of the cash to the people in Marfa. The letter read as follows:

    My dear Captain Matlack August 18, 1919

    Major C. C. Smith, 8th Cavalry, and Mr. H. M. Fennell, V. P., Marfa National Bank, bearer of this letter, take to you $15,000 ransom money demanded for the return of the aviators, Lieutenants Peterson and Davis. This money has been advanced through the Marfa National Bank by the prominent ranchmen and citizens of this and surrounding counties, subscribed yesterday afternoon within five minutes after the news of the demands of the bandits were announced at a camp meeting.

    Very truly yours,
    George T. Langhorne, Colonel, US Cavalry

    Stacy C. Hinkle, *Wings and Saddles: The Air and Cavalry Punitive Expedition of 1919* (El Paso: Texas Western Press, 1967), 14.

    According to Means, "Matlack was a native of Kentucky who joined the army at age eighteen as a private. This was in 1898. He served in Puerto Rico, the Philippines, Wyoming, Arizona, New Mexico, Fort Bliss and the Big Bend. He attained the rank of First Sergeant and was commissioned a second lieutenant in 1917. While in the Big Bend, he was stationed at Ruidosa, Indio, Pilares and Candelaria." 233.

    Hinkle continues Matlack's history: "In the mid-1900's, Matlack retired with a glowing record of army service. During World War II, he worked as a guard in a defense plant, then returned to his farm in Kentucky. Having survived nearly forty years of dangerous cavalry campaigning, he died of injuries received in a fall from an apple tree." 54–55.

Chapter 12

51. Renteria must have been a frightening character, with his cork leg and a hook in place of one of his hands. Other accounts claimed that Renteria was killed that day, and never seen again.

52. Major Yancey was tried in a military court-martial for allowing four Mexican nationals to be shot when taken as prisoners in the Second Punitive Expedition. He was accused of making false statements, ordering witnesses to make false statements, and turning military prisoners over to civilian scouts. He was reduced to the rank of captain, but pardoned by President Wilson in 1922. Thompson, 195.

Addendum

53. Both Robert Keil and Jimmy Everett lived in Tucson, Arizona, in later years. According to Means, Jim Everett died in Tucson, Arizona, March 11, 1975, and Robert Keil died in June 1971. 108.

54. The use of the term "speaks fluent Mexican" seems odd. It isn't clear whether Keil is using the word "Mexican" interchangeably with "Spanish," or acknowledging the Spanish spoken on the border would have been a dialect.

55. A manta was a large clean square of white canvas (twelve feet by twelve feet) that was laid on the ground, piled with cargo, and then lashed to the mule's back. Smithers, 29.

56. "The studs," derived from the term "stud" or "stallion," was used to describe when a mule become ornery, or rebellious, a state where he would do anything but what he was expected to do.

57. Often the two mines are confused, but in fact, silver was mined at Shafter (Thompson, 192), now a ghost town between Marfa and Presidio/Ojinaga, and quicksilver was mined at Terlingua, now a ghost town near the entrance to Big Bend National Park (See Kenneth Baxter Ragsdale, *Quicksilver: Terlingua and the Chisos Mining Company* [College Station, Texas: Texas A&M University Press, 1976]).

Bibliography

Atkin, Ronald. *Revolution! Mexico 1910–1920.* New York: The John Day Company, 1970.

Cox, Mike. *Texas Ranger Tales II*. Plano, Tx: Republic of Texas Press, 1999.

Gómez, Arthur R. "The Glen Springs-Boquillas Raid Reconsidered: Diplomatic Intrigue on the Rio Grande." *Journal of Big Bend Studies* 4 (1992): 97–113.

Hinkle, Stacy C. *Wings and Saddles: The Air and Cavalry Punitive Expedition of 1919.* El Paso: Texas Western Press, 1967.

Justice, Glenn. *Revolution on the Rio Grande: Mexican Raids and Army Pursuits, 1916–1919.* El Paso: Texas Western Press, 1992.

Means, Joyce. *Pancho Villa Days at Pilares.* Rev. ed. Tucson, Ariz. (306 W. President St., Tucson 85714), 1994.

Montejano, David. *Anglos and Mexicans in the Making of Texas 1836–1986.* Austin: University of Texas Press, 1987.

Ragsdale, Kenneth Baxter. *Quicksilver: Terlingua and the Chisos Mining Company.* College Station, Tx: Texas A&M University Press, 1976.

Ramos, Mary G., ed. *Texas Almanac of 2000–2001*. Dallas: *The Dallas Morning News*, 1999.

Raun, Gerald G. "The National Guard on the Border and One Soldier's Viewpoint." *Journal of Big Bend Studies* 6 (1994): 123–137.

Taylor, P. S. *An American-Mexican Frontier: Nueces County, Texas.* Chapel Hill: University of North Carolina Press, 1934. Reprint, New York: Russell and Russell, 1971.

Thompson, Cecelia. *History of Marfa and Presidio County, Volume Two, 1901–1946.* Austin: Nortex Press, 1985.

Warnock, Barton H. *Wildflowers of the Big Bend Country.* Alpine, Tx: Sul Ross State University, 1970.